Preaching About Crises in the Community

Preaching About ... Series

Preaching About Crises in the Community

Samuel D. Proctor

The Westminster Press
Philadelphia

© 1988 Samuel D. Proctor

Unless otherwise identified, scripture quotations are from the King James Version of the Bible.

Scripture quotations marked RSV are from the Revised Standard Version of the Bible, copyrighted 1946, 1952, © 1971, 1973 by the Division of Christian Education of the National Council of the Churches of Christ in the U.S.A., and are used by permission.

Book design by Gene Harris

First edition

Published by The Westminster Press®
Philadelphia, Pennsylvania

PRINTED IN THE UNITED STATES OF AMERICA

9 8 7 6 5 4 3 2 1

Library of Congress Cataloging-in-Publication Data

Proctor, Samuel D.
    Preaching about crises in the community / Samuel D. Proctor.
— 1st ed.

        p.   cm. — (Preaching about— series)
    Bibliography: p.
    ISBN 0–664–24084–4 (pbk.)

    1. Preaching.   2. Christianity and politics.   3. Church and the world.   4. Church and social problems—United States.   I. Title.
II. Series.
BV4235.P7P76 1988
251—dc19   87–17195
                                                                            CIP

Dedicated with
grateful memory
to
Joseph Pius Barbour
John Malcus Ellison
and
John Bennett Henderson

Contents

Acknowledgments

Every preacher who cherishes the privilege of declaring the gospel enjoys sharing those innermost stirrings of the soul and the mental challenge that preaching evokes, especially when it is responding to pressing community needs. These lectures resulted from several of my efforts to do just that.

In the spring semesters of 1986 and 1987 I was privileged to be a visiting lecturer in homiletics at the Union Theological Seminary in New York City and Princeton Theological Seminary in New Jersey, respectively. Notes for those classes, mainly, were reworked to form the basic outlines that follow.

Also, in preparing sermons for the 1986 Sprunt Lectures at the Union Theological Seminary in Virginia, and the 1987 Earle Lectures at the Pacific School of Religion in Berkeley, California, several of these topics were addressed.

The chapters on community began as a Baccalaureate Sermon at Boston University in 1985. Other chapters were prepared as lectures for preachers and seminary students as a Rauschenbusch Lecture at Colgate Rochester Divinity School/Bexley Hall/Crozer Theological Seminary in Rochester, New York; for

1987 lectures at Andover Newton Theological School and Harvard Divinity School in Massachusetts; earlier for the Lutheran Theological Seminary at Philadelphia, the Howard University Divinity School in Washington, D.C., the School of Theology of Virginia Union University in Richmond, and the Interdenominational Theological Center in Atlanta.

Because of a deep and long-standing indebtedness of mine to the late Harry Emerson Fosdick for helping me to defend my theology from the assaults of biblical criticism and scientism, I was especially grateful to give the lecture on the "voice from within" at the 1986 preaching convocation in his honor at the Union Theological Seminary in New York City.

Friends of many years who have attended the Massanetta Bible Conferences in Virginia and those who attended the 1984 Princeton Pastors Conference will recognize much of this material.

To all of those who made such opportunities available to me I extend my sincere appreciation. I owe special thanks to Lorrain Smoller, my dutiful typist, and to my wife, Bessie, and our sons for the time they allowed me to pursue the labors listed above.

S.D.P.

1

What Makes
This Ground Holy?

**Put off thy shoes from off thy feet; for the place whereon
thou standest is holy ground.**

—Exodus 3:5

The preacher has the unique responsibility to stand
tall in the midst of our moral confusion, our spiritual estrangement, and our lost opportunities and to
declare that God is with us in our situation. News
commentators, columnists, analysts, and television
anchor people may make plain what our condition
is, with meticulous detail and fastidious accuracy,
but no one except the preacher is expected to proclaim that above, around, beneath, and throughout this deep, dark morass lies the pervasive purpose of a loving and caring God. The good news the
preacher announces is that no matter how hopeless
or unpromising our situation may be, we are never
in it alone. This good news resounds throughout
the Bible.

Holy Ground Often Looks Unpromising

When Moses was in Midian tending Jethro's flock, the situation was far from perfect. Moses was a fugitive, because he had slain an Egyptian, and he was trying to make a new life for himself among the Midianites. Meanwhile he was aware of the continuing suffering of his people at the cruel hands of Pharaoh in Egypt. He did not feel at home in Midian. He felt his circumstances had to change, for better or for worse. In the midst of this uncertainty, Moses was drawn aside by the sight of a burning bush and there began his long encounter with God. He was told to take off his shoes, for the ground on which he stood was holy ground.

Surrounding him was rather ordinary natural scenery. Nothing about this dry and desolate wilderness territory looked holy. But because God had brought time and eternity, earth and heaven, the real and the ethereal together at that place and at that moment, it was holy ground. Moses was called to go down into Egypt and tell Pharaoh to let God's people go. Wherever God's presence is felt and known, and wherever God's purpose is affirmed, the ground is holy ground indeed.

Today, we are not likely to see a bush burning on the slopes of Mount Horeb in the Midian desert, and neither are we likely to be called to go into a hostile country to liberate our enslaved sisters and brothers. But we are called by the crises of our times to be aware of the needs of people in our communities. We have not found out why our youth, the privileged and the educated as well as the marginal and the deprived, have given themselves in such large numbers to drug use and addiction, with the violent crime, prostitution, and waste of brainpower and talent that follow. We cannot find a way of establishing the values that under-gird and sustain marriage and family living. We cannot find the political will to house our homeless, to feed our hungry, to care for our mentally ill, and to protect our street people, who are powerless and alone. We have not been able to make schooling attractive to masses of children who have grown up in places where education was largely neglected, and we are now facing a growing underclass that is unemployed, ill-housed, angry, and dangerous. This is no Midian desert, but when God calls the preacher to lead the people into an awareness of these needs, and the people respond, the ground is holy ground indeed. God's involvement is reaffirmed.

This is the good news—that God is more than a physical and chemical process, more than an ancient tribal deity, more than the answer to a metaphysical riddle, resolution of a syllogism, or the first cause and prime mover of the universe. The good news is that God is infinite in wisdom, love, and power. Besides being the monitor of the physical world, God is the guardian of the moral world. God is not distant and removed, but near and involved.

God has conferred upon us intelligence and freedom, and the cosmic natural order follows the patterns established by the hand of our great Creator. Moreover, because God is a free, volitional, and purposive being, and we are created in that same image, we are capable of responding to God's leadership in the world.

Indeed, it may be difficult to imagine that God has a stake in a heated school board election, a local no-smoking ordinance, a street lined with "adult" theaters, an alcoholic sleeping all night over a steam vent on a city street, a bribery scandal, or an overcrowded jail that has become a crime school; in the lack of recreational facilities for youth or food kitchens for the hungry. But if the God we serve is the One revealed in Jesus of Galilee, if our God was the One who bent low over demon-possessed children, who stopped funeral processions to comfort weeping widows, who heard the wailing of blind Bartimeus on the Jericho road and sent the paralytic from the Pool of Bethesda running rejoicing, then this God cares about us wherever we are, and when we heed this Presence the ground is holy ground.

How Do We Recognize Holy Ground?

However, not all preachers will find it comfortable or inviting to lift up the needs of the community regularly in their preaching. Many will fail to identify the preacher's role with that of Moses or to recognize that the ground where they serve could become holy ground. Even so, many are already deeply committed to this form of ministry and have developed real skill in raising awareness and in leading people into constructive community action. Some have even made this theme their total preaching ministry, at the cost of neglecting basic evangelical emphases and the spiritual nurture of the people.

Others, no doubt, have recognized the claim of community concerns upon their preaching but, to avoid possible repercussions, have allowed the worshipers to remain "at ease in Zion." They have then chosen to preserve their popularity and acceptance, and to enjoy the compliments of those who find it pleasant to be left unchallenged by the unmet needs and failures of the community. This stance is common and falls far short of the high calling of the role of the prophet of God in the Judeo-Christian tradition.

God's prophets considered their own comfort and popularity as secondary and accepted the proclamation of the Word as primary.

If one grants that the preacher, as a prophet of God, has the responsibility of recognizing God's leadership, viewing the community through the eyes of Christ, applying basic Christian moral calipers to the concerns of the people, and lifting these concerns in preaching, how does one go about doing these things? Is there a special way? We are not living in the days of Elijah, Obadiah, Nathan, Ahab, or David. We live in a money economy, not a bartering one; our people must have cash to live. We are mostly urban, not agrarian, and even our rural areas are influenced by television, radio, and the print media. Our cosmology is different, and the universe is larger and longer lasting than that assumed in the biblical view. God has more different kinds of people to watch over than the biblical personalities knew about. Our morality places higher expectations on us. We cannot accept the kind of killing and revenge that Saul, David, and Solomon took for granted as approved by God. We have rejected the secondary status of women and children that the Old Testament and Paul accepted. We do not condone slavery. The identification of wealth as a sign of God's favor is not a part of our theology.

Jesus lived a short while in an area not much larger than the state of Delaware, without a wife or children, without a home or a car, without a mortgage, life insurance, a pension, or health coverage. He lived under a dictatorship, and the people had no responsibility for self-government except in religious matters. Human behavior was ruled by tradition, religious obedience, and intuition, without the influence of organized, highly financed peddlers of ideas. There was no television, ever-present and operated for profit, pervading society with values reflecting hedonistic and narcissistic views of life.

Holy Ground Then and Now

Recognizing the difference between our world and that of the Bible, what things remain constant? First, there are commitment and courage. The record shows that the true prophets were obedient to the intuitive revealed message that God laid on their hearts, and this, not personal popularity, became their priority.

When Elijah saw how young Ahab had been captivated by Jezebel and had forsaken his own religion and built an altar to Baal, he risked life and limb to correct this abuse and began a campaign to establish Jehovah's position as the one true God. It was not easy. One of the most dramatic scenes in the Bible is the meeting of Ahab and Elijah described in 1 Kings 18.

Obadiah, a God-fearing man and Ahab's chief steward, had been sent out to look for some grass to feed the herds, which had suffered from a drought. While Obadiah was roaming around he came upon Elijah and fell on his face before the prophet, asking if it was really he. Elijah acknowledged who he was and told Obadiah to go back to the wicked king's house and announce that Elijah was in the area.

Obadiah begged the prophet not to send such a message by him. Although Obadiah had already shown courage by hiding a hundred prophets of Israel from Ahab and Jezebel in a cave and sending them bread and water secretly, he was unwilling to announce Elijah's arrival. Elijah was so hated by Ahab that even the messenger of his coming was in jeopardy.

But when Elijah told Obadiah that he would go before Ahab unannounced, Obadiah changed his mind and made the announcement to the king. When Ahab and Elijah met, the greeting Ahab gave to Elijah expressed all the credentials a prophet needs. In the light of Ahab's infidelity toward God and his bold betrayal of his people, so threatening to God's prophets that they had hidden in caves, what an honor, what a distinction, what a tribute, what a moment of esteem and recognition it is when Ahab says to Elijah, "Art thou he that troubleth Israel?" (1 Kings 18:17). In other words, Are you the one we have been hearing about? Are you the one who questions my behavior? Are you the one who dares to challenge me and my conduct?

Where Ahab, with his guilt, met Elijah and heard Elijah tell him to his face that he had forsaken the commandments and followed Baal, there we find another patch of holy ground. God, through the prophet Elijah, has entered the flow of history once again and through the prophet has manifested concern for what is happening to the people.

As the preacher stays close to his or her Bible, there will appear one instance after another in which God gives direction and strength, so that the moral and spiritual dimensions of a situation may be addressed. One finds evidence over and over that the moral earnestness of a Holy God stirs the soul of the sincere servant of God. In the face of blatant wrongdoing, in the face of human suffering, in the face of palpable injustice, in the face of neglect of the helpless and abuse of the powerless, in the face of unmet needs that jeopardize the maintenance of a minimum standard of human decency, the prophet finds the courage to speak. The ground becomes holy ground, and the people who love the Lord are strengthened in their faith and edified by living the Christian life when they witness God's prophet reflecting such love and concern.

In addition to comfort and courage, God gives wisdom to the prophet. Preaching the good news in response to community concerns is more than joining the bandwagon for one popular issue after another. Rather, it is seriously responding to a situation where prophetic insight must be applied, in very delicate and uncomfortable situations.

Nathan was probably embarrassed to remind King David of his adultery. Surely this was not a popular thing to do. If Nathan had been a frequent luncheon guest in the palace or a partner of David in some sport like fishing, hunting, or golfing, if Nathan were known to be David's crony, one of his clerical sycophants, it would have been even more difficult for Nathan to tell David how wrong he was. Such familiarity with royalty tends to breed a personal loyalty that colors the entire relationship. In such a situation the prophet feels less like a prophet of God and more like a member of the king's court, more inclined to view the world through the king's eyes than through the eyes of God.

Nathan had known David well and had persuaded him to build a house of worship, a house of cedar, where the ark could be safely lodged. So from this position of trust Nathan found it necessary to confront David when he had committed a terrible offense.

David had coveted the wife of his soldier, Uriah the Hittite; he had had her brought to him and conceived a child with her. Then he sent for her soldier husband, pretended to be his friend, offered him the courtesies of the king's house, and had him sent to the thickest and bloodiest battle in order to have him killed. Finally, David fabricated a lie to cover up his mischief.

The prophet Nathan learned of this, confronted David, and brought him to repentance. Later, when David was old and feeble, this same Nathan went before him to gain assurance that Solomon, the son of Bathsheba, widow of Uriah the Hittite, would be given his rightful place on the throne. David had married Bathsheba, and Solomon was her second child by him. In this entire matter, Nathan represented the moral authority of God.

Throughout this account, we find in the ancient story a reminder that the prophet has a special role and function. The prophetic message has intrinsic authenticity because it is no respecter of persons but represents the justice, the righteousness, and the love of God in all human situations.

Today's preacher must transpose the message of God from the ancient world of goats, tents, still waters, green pastures, burning bushes, and camel caravans to our world of laser beams, electron microscopes, fast foods, credit cards, and the Super Bowl. The scenery changes, but the human situation remains strangely the same.

Responding to God's Initiative Today

When we fail to address these concerns, they do not go away. They become compounded and are exploited for the benefit of someone who gains from the neglect. In America we are now being inundated with the problem of drug abuse. Throughout the country the drug industry operates with sophisticated distribution routes, preparation centers, protection strategies, bribery networks, quick bail-bond arrangements, and the laundering of large sums of money. It represents an entire underground economy and employment system. Personnel are trained in chemistry, weaponry, automobile registration, police tactics, court procedures, and state and federal legal codes. It is common knowledge that selling crack can yield an income higher than practicing medicine or programming computers. Of course, such a career may come to an abrupt end in a prison term or a homicide, but it is ever so seductive to someone looking for a quick release from poverty.

The drug epidemic did not begin at this level of operation. It was first a small-scale, isolated phenomenon found mostly among desperate persons in the ghettos, in dingy bars where one moved up from alcohol to reefers to heroin. We read about it, never imagining that it could spread to our own kitchens and living rooms. Now, many otherwise successful families are wondering where they were when all this happened.

The silence on this matter was deafening. It seemed like an issue among the poor, the rock singers, the motorcycle gangs, the adult-movie goers, and the bearded ones, but not an issue for mainline churches and family people. But when we fail to address a concern it does not go away. The drug industry is fostering crime at a staggering rate. Automobile thefts, house robberies, street muggings, credit card counterfeiting, and police bribery are all aggravated by the paralyzing craving for a fix and the need for a heavy cash flow to maintain a habit costing hundreds of dollars a day.

Anyone who lives or works near this drug environment senses something demonic about it that defies easy analysis. Anyone whose heart allows him or her to deliver a twelve-year-old into the drug dungeon where the chances of escape are minuscule cannot be dealt with lightly. Anyone who can kill a seventeen-year-old boy in cold blood, in broad daylight on a busy street, for an overdue payment on a drug delivery has turned away from all that is right and decent in the world.

The total absorption that the drug habit requires, the constant quest for money and privacy, and the inability to concentrate on other goals with any measure of consistency all mean that one is truly demon-possessed.

This community concern stares us all in the face. The magnitude of it, the volumes of money involved, the depth of the commitment that it calls for demand the best efforts of all caring Christians.

This is not only a police issue. It is also a school matter because drugs have penetrated our campuses and schoolyards. It concerns legislative bodies and those volunteer agencies that are holding a finger in the dike. But when we see how drug addiction drags young women into prostitution, how it destroys talent and mental ability, how it divides families and corrupts the police and the courts, we have a massive moral issue. The preacher must address this in the light of God's love for every person and the dignity that has been conferred upon all human life by the enfolding of the person of God in human flesh. The good news is that God bent low, and visited our condition, and thereby elevated us above instinctive animal survival behavior and made us "little less than God" (Ps. 8:5, RSV). Our imperative is that something is happening here to God's children that should never have reached such proportions and should be eradicated. When the good news confronts this issue, we are on holy ground.

Lest we think the task is too great, we can be encouraged by what happened when the black people were emancipated. Professor James McPherson of Prince-

ton, in *The Abolitionist Legacy,* has described the development of secondary schools and colleges throughout
the South to serve the newly freed black population.
The South was ravaged. Hatred was rife. Blacks
roamed around in a daze. But soon there emerged a
secondary school in almost every county and at least
one college in every southern state. Presbyterians,
Baptists, Methodists, Episcopalians, Congregational-
ists, Lutherans, and smaller groups preached to their
people the need for Christians to step into this moral
chasm and answer a crying need.

From that effort has grown the family of private
colleges now making up the United Negro College
Fund, along with such institutions as Howard, Hamp-
ton, and Lincoln universities. Some federal funds were
provided from the Freedmen's Bureau during the
1860s and 1870s, but college development was mostly
a project of Christian persuasion and missionary
dimes and dollars. A student of American history who
did not know this story would be faced with a great
enigma: How did black people emerge from slavery
and, in such a hostile climate, move steadily to find
their place in U.S. society? Where did their physicians,
lawyers, principals, coaches, choir directors, teachers,
social workers, preachers, and politicians come from
so fast, in spite of the restrictions, denials, and obsta-
cles facing them? Well, some preachers did not allow
the matter to rest. They preached to this concern and
God gave a rich harvest. Things are not yet what they
should be, but the distance covered already is due in
great part to the courageous and dedicated group of
white teachers who poured out of church colleges
across the North into the cities and towns of the South
following the Civil War. They came in the spirit of
Christian service, and they changed those dusty roads
and muddy hollows into holy ground.

We know what happened when the preachers were on time; the results in our nation for everyone's benefit were enormous. Now, in education itself as well as the drug problem, we face a concern that calls us with the same urgency. We have an underclass forming in our country. The gap between those who are making it and those who are being pushed out of the race is widening. We have heard of the hungry and the homeless. In the 1960s we made a large effort to reach the poor. But we find that emergency measures are not that effective. We need to reach children early with good education, wholesome recreation, and intellectually challenging experiences to bring an entire generation out of poverty and dependency, out of alienation and estrangement, out of darkness into the marvelous light.

In our knowledge-intensive society, if we allow the middle class to escape to private schools and convert public schools into armed camps, within a generation we will have one fifth of the population locked out of meaningful employment, angry and frustrated, resented by the tax-paying majority, easy bait for single-solution politicians, and suicidal in their search for quick remedies. This problem is easily overlooked. It is like a disease with silent symptoms. If we are not close to these failing segments of society, we are not aware of the threat. But the victims will surface as young adults, semiliterate, ashamed, afraid, and disgusted by their inability to function.

This is more than a social and economic issue. Those who observe a life that has missed many of the precious growth opportunities that most of us have experienced know it hurts deeply. When one sees a mind wasted it *is* a terrible thing! God has equipped us mentally and psychologically for growth and freedom, to become aware of choice and options, to live in the subjunctive mood—aware of the possible. With this awareness, this freedom, this choice we become moral beings able to choose to seek the Lord. But for persons unaware of choice, options, or freedom who are left to live by glandular and neurological necessity, the results are frightening.

The preacher is called to shed the light of the good news upon this community concern. God sent Christ to show us the way to the abundant life. In modern terms this means more than a life sustained by physical necessities. The abundant life is one of self-determination, of freedom to choose the high road or the low. The abundant life overflows with creativity and spiritual renewal, with a source of hope that is inexhaustible because it comes from God.

When we cry out for excellence, safety, and support in our schools for the sake of those who are there, the possibility of the abundant life is opened for them. When we preach on this we are on holy ground.

Finding the Adequacy to Respond

When the moment to preach on a community concern arrives and the need is clearly apparent, we may find ourselves consumed by feelings of inadequacy. When Moses discovered that God was pointing him toward a real need, his first response was a feeling of inadequacy: "Who am I, that I should go?" (Ex. 3:11). This is like saying, "Can't you find someone else, someone closer to the situation, someone better able to deal with this? Why me?" Some issues that demand our attention are so nebulous, so amorphous, so difficult to grasp and to assess that we wish we did not have to deal with them at all. The question of gay rights, for example, brings out our concern for Christian family stability and the moral direction that young people need, as well as our compassion for all of God's children and our commitment to justice and fairness. Between these two sets of values it is not easy to be forthright and consistent. Because of this ambivalence, the issue generates great divisiveness and controversy. Little wonder that when the preacher is asked to address it, the first words that may come out are "Why me?"

Our feelings of inadequacy may be related also to our doubts about our authority. Will anyone listen? Moses protested to God, "Behold, when I come unto the children of Israel, and shall say unto them, the God of your fathers hath sent me unto you . . . they shall say to me, What is his name?" (Ex. 3:13). In every religious affiliation the authority of the clergy has been eroded, partly owing to the irrelevance of many of the burdensome theological anachronisms; partly to the lukewarm moral positions that churches have taken and their silence where their witness was needed; partly because our influence has been supplanted by modernity, the scientific and technological explosion, and the media. We are no longer at the center of society as the churches were in the earlier decades of this century. Many of our great churches are boarded up or converted to other uses. Many of our downtown "First" churches are poorly attended and exist on old endowments. It is understandable that one may feel that to speak or not to speak is pointless. Who will listen?

The last protest that Moses made, that he was not able, is also familiar. "I am not good at this. I am better at Bible teaching, counseling, church administration, or fund raising, but not at dealing with community concerns." Moses said, "I am not eloquent . . . I am slow of speech, and of a slow tongue" (Ex. 4:10). Many feel that, both by temperament and by experience and talent, they should leave community concerns to more competent voices. While this may be true, it is perhaps more the case that one lacks infor-mation—familiarity with the issue—or commitment, or both.

Illustrative of social distance and lack of familiarity was the question asked me by a TV reporter at the annual concert of the New York Philharmonic Orches-tra held in the Abyssinian Baptist Church in Harlem. "Why do you bother to have this every year? Do your people really appreciate this?" Even as he talked, six-teen hundred persons were elbow to elbow, leaving the auditorium; the applause and the encores had given solid evidence of their appreciation, and earlier in the day, at the dress rehearsal, the room had been filled beyond capacity by schoolchildren and senior citizens.

His experience was so narrow, his views so provin-cial, his information so sketchy, the stereotypes in his mind so indelible that he thought people in Harlem had no taste for this music, which had come from every continent, had been played for ages in every culture, and reflected the total range of human experi-ence.

Some preachers have lived in such an isolated seg-ment of society, protected from problem areas and problem people, that they do indeed feel inadequate in addressing community concerns. One wonders how they relate to Jesus, who found his way into the thick of human need and spent his entire three years of preaching and healing demonstrating God's concern for marginal people.

Ultimately, a deepened commitment will go far to correct our inadequacies. If our commitment to Christ is formal, perfunctory, and thin, our inadequacies will remain glaring. But as we get closer to him in love, in service, and in obedience, we begin to increase our capacity to respond to community concerns. This should be a growing and deepening experience, following Christ's leadership into the corners of life where hurt souls have sought refuge. He was so attuned to their needs that without looking he knew from a touch that someone hurt had reached for the hem of his garment.

Such commitment may cause us to raise some questions and point out needs that may sound strange to our congregations, but this is what it means to be sent by God, to be the herald of the kingdom of righteousness. This is why John the Baptist seemed so strange to those who were bound to the status quo. Jesus asked them, concerning John's presence and preaching, "What did you go out into the wilderness to behold? A reed shaken by the wind? Why then did you go out? To see a man clothed in soft raiment? Behold, those who wear soft raiment are in kings' houses. Why then did you go out? To see a prophet? Yes, I tell you, and more than a prophet" (Matt. 11:7–9, RSV).

Somewhere on a scale with John the Baptist at one end and, at the other, the nonchalant accommodation we are so tempted to make to assuage the guilt, the callousness, the indifference of people who have grown numb to human need, each one of us can find a place as a preacher on community concerns. But with a deeper commitment as a preacher of the good news, we will discern the relevance of the gospel to these community concerns and bring the people into a richer, more meaningful experience of the love of Christ and of God's purpose in the world. Wherever this happens, whether in a Gothic cathedral or in a clapboard church on a little rise against the quiet woods, the ground is holy ground.

2

Where Do We Begin When Values Are in Flux?

In those days there was no king in Israel, but every man did that which was right in his own eyes.
—Judges 17:6

As we preachers approach community concerns in the light of the good news of the gospel, our initial assumption is that everyone shares our point of view. The good news proclaims a specific person in history and a moral perspective demonstrated in the lives of many people. Moreover, it calls for a certain relationship to God that rejects pretense and sham, hypocrisy and cynicism, deceit and chicanery. Our first pulpit assignment is to make the congregation aware of the content, the body, the meaning of the gospel. It is unique and it has salience. It is not simply a warm, cozy feeling about God, a palliative for our guilt and a placebo for our pain. It offers a restored and reconciled relationship with God. The good news tells us how this relationship is possible for everyone and how earnestly God is seeking our restoration and reconciliation. We may never reach perfection in this relationship, but we live in faith, and God's grace and mercy sustain us in the whole process.

The Climate of Moral Ambivalence

When we approach a community concern from this experience and background, we discover that the values derived from our Christian experience are in confrontation with a cacophony of strange sounds and symbols about what is good and what is bad, what is right and what is wrong. Then we know what it feels like to be a voice crying in the wilderness. The anonymity of urban life has removed most persons from their moral support system of familiar faces, customs, rituals, and scenes. The secular thrust, the competitiveness, the insecurity, the mobility, the crass materialism of our society are all incompatible with the moral and spiritual tone of the good news.

Recently our attention has been drawn sharply to the appalling statistics on teenage pregnancies. It is an epidemic, especially among the urban poor. We have wrung our hands and gritted our teeth over this one, because we see it as a sign that family life is seriously threatened. Yet at the same time network television announces, without an eyebrow raised, the birth of a baby to an unmarried millionaire tennis star and an unmarried glamorous actress. We have grown accustomed to news of the wealthy and famous freely cohabiting without benefit of clergy, and rich divorcées opting to bear children by their unmarried lovers. Another national news commentator presents a spokesperson from a women's college advocating the virtues of a school that grants support to the cause of lesbians. In the chapel of one institution two women married each other. These instances illustrate

the state of flux in which we find the values of our
society.

Very few traditional values have remained fixed. We
are reminded of that verse in the Book of Judges: "In
those days there was no king in Israel, but every man
did that which was right in his own eyes" (Judg. 17:6).
Even such basic values as honesty and truthfulness are
so flagrantly violated in high places that it appears we
are in a moral vacuum. Recently the confidential aide
to a large-city mayor was discovered holding a $78,-
000 position that would ordinarily require college and
professional training. This young man had lied about
his training, claiming to have a college degree he did
not in fact possess. At the same time schoolteachers
were fighting to get an $18,000 starting salary.

On the national scene, military spending accounts
for one half of the budget, and it is common knowledge that many of the nation's major corporations
have virtually abandoned all sense of restraint in padding defense contract expenditures and overcharging
the government at ridiculously high percentages, 700
and 800 percent on many items. Some have been fined
but most have offered vague and deceptive explana-
tions, and the public has been quieted.

A judge of over twenty years' tenure was indicted
and sentenced in one of the largest cities in the country for habitually taking bribes in cases involving organized crime, drug dealers, murderers, car thieves, and
bank robbers. The leader of a major political party in
our largest city committed suicide with a bread knife
as an investigation about corruption in city government drew closer and closer to him. We are in a moral
vacuum. How can the preacher assert a moral position
when the assumptions on which such an assertion is
based are shattered?

Something has gone awry. Values are in flux and it

is not easy to find a moral consensus. Our society boasts of individual liberty, due process of law, the rights of detainees to remain silent and not incriminate themselves, and protection from unreasonable punishment, search, and seizure. Moreover, our freedom of speech, press, worship, and assembly provides a multitude of privileges that can be abused, such as the avalanche of filthy movies, books, music, magazines, and vulgar television programs. These freedoms were established at a time when it was assumed that the country had a moral fabric woven out of the Judeo-Christian tradition, the lofty principles that were the legacy of the Athens of Pericles, the Renaissance, the Enlightenment, the Reformation, and English common law.

Senator Robert Y. Hayne of South Carolina debated Daniel Webster in the Senate chamber on January 26, 1830, on the question of the preservation of the union versus the right of a state to secede. As the story goes, Hayne made a devastating attack on Webster and the North. But when Webster rebutted he was so moving, so spontaneously eloquent, that Hayne stopped him later in the cloakroom to ask how he could be so well prepared with no notice. Webster replied that he did not need any notice. He said that as he listened to Hayne's attack on the Union, everything he had ever read in the Bible, in the Constitution, and in the Declaration of Independence came before him in "panoramic array," and when he needed "a thunderbolt he just reached out and grabbed it as it went smoking by." He drew on the nation's reservoir of moral reserves.

Today, those reserves are low and dangerously shallow. In fact it is stylish to boast that one has "no moral position" on anything. It has come to be antisocial to affirm a moral position and a sign of sophistication to be amoral. This is the atmosphere in which the preacher must declare the good news that God has acted on a cosmic scale, in a unique manner, absolutely and finally, in Jesus Christ to reconcile the human race to its divine Creator. This is the kind of society that is spread before the preacher, and he or she must lift up one piece of it after another and examine it in the light of the gospel.

The preacher speaks for God and not as a casual observer. Preachers are agents of God's purpose, and God has not given up on the world. Preachers stand in the procession of prophets among whom Isaiah stood also when he cried out:

> "The Spirit of the Lord GOD is upon me;
> Because the LORD hath anointed me
> To preach good tidings unto the meek;
> He hath sent me to bind up the broken-hearted,
> To proclaim liberty to the captives,
> And the opening of the prison to them that are
>   bound;
> To appoint unto them that mourn in Zion,
> To give unto them beauty for ashes,
> The oil of joy for mourning,
> The garment of praise for the spirit of heaviness;
> That they might be called Trees of righteousness,
> The planting of the LORD, that he might be
>   glorified."
>
> —Isaiah 61:1, 3

The Good News and Moral Direction

The preacher proclaims the gift of God in Jesus Christ, and there is no moral ambiguity here. We do not have another theory like Kant's categorical imperative, another school of thought like the Milesian philosophers, another long allegory like Dante's *Inferno* or Bunyan's *Pilgrim's Progress,* great as they are. We have a living Lord; we have the biography of a real person, one who was "in all points tempted like as we are, yet without sin." We have a warm-blooded, muscular, human example, a life nurtured in the womb of a woman, born in a Bethlehem barn, raised in a family with brothers and sisters; who hungered, thirsted, cried, and slept as we do; who was alone in the desert for forty days and forty nights canvassing his options, sorting out the program for his ministry, settling on his agenda, and fighting off the devil; who was misunderstood by his family, betrayed by his disciples, and killed on a cruel cross by his enemies. But God would not let death hold him. And now we sing rejoicing:

> O for a thousand tongues to sing
> Our great Redeemer's praise,
> The glories of our God and King,
> The triumphs of his grace.

This is the good news, that God has acted. God gave us the moral model in Jesus Christ. So while there may be confusion about our values, this confusion is allayed and dissipated when we lift up the person and the message of Jesus. When we approach community concerns in the light of his life and teachings, there is a cleansing of the atmosphere, a steadying of our purpose, a correction in our course of action, a feeling of confidence that what we are doing is not whimsical or capricious and without foundation, but based upon the lasting and universal divine will. And somehow, when we fix our minds to follow the leadership of Christ, we hear the echo of what God said to Joshua: "As I was with Moses, so I will be with thee: I will not fail thee, nor forsake thee. Be strong and of a good courage . . . ; be not afraid, neither be thou dismayed; for the LORD thy God is with thee whithersoever thou goest" (Josh. 1:5–6, 9).

What are the principles, the guideposts, the criteria that we should follow if we are to preach in the midst of this moral morass and respond to the concerns of the community in the light of God's good news in Jesus Christ? Where do we begin our assessment of how the good news applies to these concerns?

The Good News and the Worth of Persons

First, the good news is person-centered; it is not focused on other aspects of our common life, such as the gross national product, or military supremacy, or racial purity, or the balance of payments, profits and losses, or the Dow Jones averages. Surely, all these may—and do—affect persons, but the focus of the good news is on enabling the blind to see, the lame to walk, the deaf to hear, the hungry to be fed, the thirsty to be given drink, the lepers to be cleansed, the sick to be healed, and the sinners to learn of the love of a merciful Father. The good news affirms the worth and the dignity of every person and seeks to bring each one into the orbit of God's power and love. "He came unto his own, and his own received him not. But as many as received him, to them gave he power to become the sons [and daughters] of God" (John 1:11–12). All other benefits in society derive their worth and are assigned their priority as they enhance the well-being of persons. Notice how Jesus frequently was in difficulty because he put the accent on the person rather than on the laws of his inherited religion. A woman was found in adultery. The law allowed her to be stoned to death. Jesus put her possibilities for renewal and restitution above the requirements of the law and said, "He that is without sin among you, let him first cast a stone at her" (John 8:7).

He told of the man on the Jericho road who had been beaten and robbed and left to die. And he told of how a priest and a Levite, who were governed by their law, passed by the man, lest some religious proscription be violated by dealing with an unknown, unclean, uncertified, apparently dead body. But a Samaritan, not bound by such laws, was free to show compassion. He bound up the wounds, took the man to the nearest town, and paid for his keep. He put the worth of the person above the requirements of the law. Jesus did not intend to destroy the minimal demands of the law, but he maximized its spirit and intent, to maintain a moral covenant between God and the people of faith. The law needed revision to meet the higher requirements of God's love for persons.

Christian moral values do not derive from some abstraction, but from the esteem and worth that Jesus placed on each human life, for God's sake and for the kingdom's sake. This estimation of the dignity of persons did not derive from the biological supremacy of *Homo sapiens,* or the unique capacity of the human brain, but rather from the intuitive awareness of ordinary bedouins like Abraham, Isaac, and Jacob that behind the orderly movement of the moon and the stars, the rhythm of the tides and the seasons, the beauty of a sunset, the strength of the eagle's wing, the songs of the thrush and the lark, there was the mind of a loving and caring God. And trusting in this God they discovered in their lives self-evident moral authentication, and God verified the truth of this divine presence in human experience. Listen to this testimony from the psalmist:

I waited patiently for the LORD;
And he inclined unto me, and heard my cry.
He brought me up also out of a horrible pit, out of the
    miry clay,
And set my feet upon a rock.

—Psalm 40:1–2

Jesus was heir to that legacy, and because of his
special role and mission he refined it, made it universal, transcended the tribal and ethnic dimensions of
Judaism, and invited all persons to share this knowledge and experience of God.

This is all still a matter of faith. It is not subject to
our narrow epistemology. We cannot prove the validity of the ethics of Jesus in a flask, in a test tube, with
a computer or a microscope. If we had a laboratory
large enough, with enough accumulated data, with
enough witnesses present, over enough generations,
the evidence would be there. But our evidence is
folded up in the history of the world since Christ came:
the awful consequences of slavery and human bond-
age, the enhancement of the position of women, the
care and concern for children, our compassion for all
who suffer hunger and want, the self-negating prac-
tices of war and vengeance, and the destructive results
of egocentricity and narcissistic approaches to life. If
hard evidence for the validity of Christian values is
difficult to establish, evidence for the *invalidity* of opposite moral approaches is abundant. It takes *more*
faith to accept the secular, materialistic, and nihilistic
understanding of life than it does to believe, "Thou
shalt love the Lord thy God with all thy heart, and
with all thy soul, and with all thy strength, and with
all thy mind; and thy neighbor as thyself" (Luke
10:27).

Following Jesus, therefore, and recognizing that
values are in flux, we hold firmly to the worth and

dignity of human life, under God, and from this basic premise derives our moral position. We look at the community and its concerns through the eyes of Christ, and thereby we get our signal on what our own position should be. Therefore we do not have contempt or hatred for young criminals who terrorize our towns. We do not respond to their crimes with a cry for the death penalty. First we try to remove them from the streets to protect the innocent; then we try to find out the influences that warped the minds of these young offenders; we try to see if *we* have failed in some way. Then, with concern for the rehabilitation of those incarcerated, we want a new beginning for those who *are* released and improved opportunities for education and moral development for those who could be headed for criminal careers. Our values are modeled after the live, historical, detailed example of Jesus.

It is very tempting to rush toward single solutions for complicated problems, to be swept up by the rhetoric of political partisans, by emotional, uninformed views that often evoke irrational and instinctive behavior, instead of the pursuit of facts and the application of the mind of Christ to even the most bothersome, unpopular, and controversial issues. Passion, inflamed by ignorance and hate, has never solved anything. Lasting and purposeful answers may require time and patience, but they have integrity and they endure.

The Good News and Our Relations with Others

Next, the good news shows us that Christ calls us to renew our relationships with others. Our faith is not private and ornamental. It must affect our involvement with others in community or it is empty and superficial. Jesus had most of his problems with dead

religion all around him. A kind of pietism and legalism
permitted unloving relationships to thrive under the
cloak of religious formalities. Christ cared about how
persons accepted their worth in the sight of God and
also how they related to other persons. The love that
the New Testament celebrates is the love that takes the
initiative in seeking to create good in the life of another. It is active love, not passive and static.

Therefore, following Christ we look at community
concerns not only in the light of the worth of persons
but also in the light of our Christian love. We are
bound by Christ's estimate of persons, as well as by his
relationship with them. And in this matter we have to
be very careful that we do not limit ourselves to one-
on-one charitable responses when it is more honest
and forthright to call for change in institutional behavior that denies the worth of persons. Genuine love
may find us doing more than preaching a hand-wring-
ing message on human hurt. The situation may call for
a sermon that alerts the congregation to an evil that
is perpetrated with a larger institutional sponsorship
that is impervious to mild suggestions.

Mainline Protestant churches are made up of persons who are generally well-off and who have only
secondhand knowledge of social victimization. The
preacher has to be responsible for informing such
congregations about situations in which the Christian
view of the worth of persons is violated. More than
that, the preacher has to inform them of how their tacit
approval of social structures makes them responsible
for such unloving and uncaring social failure. This
may not be easy, but the skill to do this, while keeping
the congregation intact and willing to learn more, can
be cultivated.

Perhaps the greater challenge is to educate persons
in such churches on the whole subject of institutional

immorality and the hurt caused by polite and respected institutions.

In some towns, for example, the old influential banks were found to be in collusion with the real estate barons to assure that persons of unwanted racial, religious, or national background could not purchase homes in certain neighborhoods. In such places it became canon, and no amount of preaching, praying, or cajoling would suffice. The moral indignation of decent people had to be aroused, and a lawsuit had to be entered to restrain such unfair behavior. The same is true about cleaning up toxic waste, scrutinizing the appointment of judges, providing better police protection, and letting bids for street repairs.

The permissiveness and port-barreling that allow the misappropriation of public funds rob the people of money to do other things for public benefit. Tolerating the abuse of lands, rivers, and air for private gain endangers the health and well-being of all people, born and unborn.

The great eighth-century prophets observed this kind of failure on a large scale, folded into social customs and crying out for a prophetic challenge. Amos prophesied punishment for Israel "because they sold the righteous for silver, and the poor for a pair of shoes" (Amos 2:6). Further, he protested, "I hate, I despise your feast days, and I will not smell in your solemn assemblies. . . . But let judgment run down as waters, and righteousness as a mighty stream" (5:21, 24).

Micah addressed the same issue—the abuses of the powerful and the mighty, and religion without fairness:

> Will the LORD be pleased with thousands of rams,
> Or with ten thousands of rivers of oil?

Shall I give my firstborn for my transgression,
The fruit of my body for the sin of my soul?
He hath showed thee, O man, what is good;
And what doth the LORD require of thee,
But to do justly, and to love mercy,
And to walk humbly with thy God? . . .
Are there yet the treasures of wickedness in the
 house of the wicked,
And the scant measure that is abominable?
Shall I count them pure with the wicked balances,
And with the bag of deceitful weights?
                                    —Micah 6:7–8, 10–11

Perhaps the most colorful condemnation of the calloused rich came from Isaiah:

The LORD will enter into judgment
With the ancients of his people, and the princes
 thereof:
For ye have eaten up the vineyard;
The spoil of the poor is in your houses.
What mean ye that ye beat my people to pieces,
And grind the faces of the poor? . . .
Moreover the LORD saith,
Because the daughters of Zion are haughty,
And walk with stretched forth necks
And wanton eyes,
Walking and mincing as they go,
And making a tinkling with their feet:
Therefore the Lord will smite with a scab
The crown of the head of the daughters of Zion.
                                    —Isaiah 3:14–17

Just as Amos, Micah, and Isaiah addressed such concerns, so the preacher with the mind of Christ disciplines himself or herself and in a timely fashion speaks the truth in love on issues where the good news cries out for a relevant application.

The Good News and Disciplined Obedience

Finally, the good news includes discipline, discipleship. The Christian life is not lukewarm or wishy-washy. The good news involves commitment. "If any man [or woman] will come after me, let him [her] . . . take up his [her] cross, and follow me" (Matt. 16:24).

No one is able to maintain this high level of loyalty consistently throughout a lifetime. We vacillate, and sometimes we are much better disciplined than at other times. There is a rat race out there that draws us into itself without our knowing. The next thing we see is that our lives, our motives, our choices have become secularized, practical, mundane, and privatized. Like Demas, we have forsaken Christ and "loved this present world" (2 Tim. 5:10). But regular and sincere worship, earnest prayer, warm fellowship with other Christians, good reading, and frequent withdrawals for reflection and quietness will pull things back into focus.

The good news sets before us a life that was obedient to God, that was attuned to the will of God, and that appropriated the power of God in love toward others and in personal moral integrity. The good news does not offer the kind of simple dichotomy that is so seductive—*either* personal righteousness *or* service to others. Jesus demonstrated simplicity, trustworthiness, honesty, and truthfulness *as well as* compassion, tenderness, and love with initiative.

Ultimately, the two parallel emphases brought him to his cross. People resented Jesus' association with the wine bibbers, the harlots, the sinners, and the publicans—the political hustlers—and they found him to be dangerously steadfast in his purpose.

Even when values are in flux, there is never any debate about the value of honesty and moral transparency. Those whose views we reject still earn our respect when they are consistent, truthful, and morally cohesive. The cross of Christ is so compelling because he accepted death for the sake of validating all that he had said and done. Therefore, persons like Gandhi, John F. Kennedy, and Martin Luther King, Jr., may have an influence and an efficacy in death that often exceed their influence in life because their martyrdom punctuated what they lived for.

In a society that tolerates retired army generals selling weapons to the government, corporations hiding contributions made to political candidates, tobacco companies hiring celebrities to deceive the public about the effects of smoking, banks laundering money for crime syndicates, medical doctors padding charges to Medicaid for treating the nation's poorest, athletes gambling on their own games, and police involved in drug traffic, anyone found holding fast to moral integrity, to consistently reliable and predictable behavior, turns out to be a rare creature.

It is a blessing to any community to have the word leak out and circulate that the Christian minister is one such person who can be trusted. It says so much for Christ when someone passing by a brick colonial church, a stone Gothic edifice, or a wooden structure with a spire pointing toward heaven on a lonely road can feel deep within that what goes on there can be believed and trusted, because what the people there say with their lips and feel in their hearts, they do, and they live with the results.

3

The Bible
and the Community Issues
Before Us

Ho, every one that thirsteth, come ye to the waters,
And he that hath no money;
Come ye, buy, and eat;
Yea, come, buy wine and milk
Without money and without price.

—Isaiah 55:1

What the preacher brings out of the Bible as preparation to meet the challenge of community needs is
not a checklist of prohibitions, not a how-to-fix-it
handbook, not a set of recipes for ready consumption,
but a wise appreciation for where the human spirit
began and how far, by the grace of God, we have
come.

The preacher has been schooled by hours of intense
Bible study to hold the long view of history while still
patiently dealing with the exigencies of the current
scene. The assurance that faith is being certain of what
we cannot see and the conviction that there is a city
whose builder and maker is God—the impending, potential, immanent kingdom of our God and of the
Christ—steady the hand and fix the mind for serious
effort. The Bible endows the preacher with a passion

for justice and with compassion for the victims of injustice; it gives the preacher the penetrating vision to see the eternal hand of God at work in the midst of our contemporaneity.

The Bible has survived the early Christian heresies, the division of the church between East and West, the mischief of unfaithful church leaders, the cataclysmic Reformation, the rise of empiricism and scientism, the industrial revolution, and the storms of communism, materialism, and humanism, and it still lies firmly in place in the midst of the tempests of modernity, urbanism, and technology. There are still words, sentences, and paragraphs in the Bible that have gathered such reverence, sanctity, and power that their sheer utterance in times of need effects an immediate response, like a change in body temperature or the pulse rate. How many times have we paused, closed our eyes, and murmured in a whisper,

> "I will lift up mine eyes unto the hills,
> From whence cometh my help,
> My help cometh from the LORD,
> Which made heaven and earth."
> —Psalm 121:1

There are passages in the scriptures whose recitations make our adrenaline accelerate, that even cause muscles to relax, hope to rise, and fears and anxieties to recede.

Because of the power of its language and the lyrical refrains found in such books as Isaiah, Psalms, Luke, John, and First and Second Corinthians, we are tempted to use the Bible like an automobile repair manual or a physician's handbook, as a catalog of magical references and prescriptions. We are inclined to snatch one phrase or another out of context and force it into the framework of our own agenda, removing it from its original meaning, imposing it upon another situation, and compelling a use that the original author never intended.

Some of the most common exploitation of believers is found in this practice, for they ascribe to the Bible an immeasurable level of trust. To have such faith misguided is a disservice of huge proportions. Imagine how churches have been divided by such questions as: What is the meaning of a certain verse of scripture? How much water does a baptism require? Who is eligible for church membership? When, how, and to whom should the Lord's Supper be served? Should there be pastors and/or bishops, deacons and/or elders? Should women be pastors? Should a pastor marry? When will Jesus return, if at all?

But the Bible cannot bear responsibility for such disputes because it was never intended to be used as a catalog of quick fixes for imponderable issues. Those writers of the sixty-six books comprising our Bible would be stunned to see how we use brief snippets from their histories, biographies, poems, dramas, letters, and hymns on which to hang thirty minutes of "this or that" every Sunday morning. They would be equally amazed at how often we toss these verses at the issues of the times and use them as substitutes for hard work and serious deliberation.

The Bible is a record of human encounter with the God of the ages, occurring in a narrow and proscribed location, over a brief stretch of time, and in a particular era. The Bible did not invent God, Christ, or the church; neither did it create sin, the sense of wonder and awe in the human spirit, the yearning for identity, the search for a home for the soul, or the longing for that transcendence here and hereafter that we call eternity. Before there was a New Testament, Jesus had grown up in Nazareth, in Joseph's carpentry shop.

Pilate had washed his hands and walked away from the choice before him, Paul had fallen from his horse, blinded by the Syrian sun, and the Holy Spirit had spoken in a thousand tongues at Pentecost.

After all that came the Bible, containing as much of it as could be written on pieces of sheepskin, as much as the alphabet could capture, as much as one could deal with using the end of an ostrich feather dipped in indigo. At least one other complete Bible was left unwritten on the scrolls but was surely etched on the hearts of men and women. The experience, the encounter, the soul's searching came first, and then came the record written by persons under divine inspiration.

These currents in the Bible carry us along (a) from a view of God as a tribal deity to the understanding of God as loving parent of all humankind in the gospels; (b) from external moral demands to internal moral controls; (c) from narrow ethnic tribalism to a genuine spiritual community; (d) from treating women, children, and servants as property to accepting them as persons; and (e) from an emphasis on the abundance of things to the attainment of the abundant life. These themes are broad and inclusive, and those who identify and follow them through the careful study of the scriptures find a tide of spiritual refreshment and strength and an inexhaustible resource for dealing with the issues and crises faced in our communities.

Therefore, as we turn to the Bible in coping with the issues before us, we are looking for the direction of the same God who was present in the pages of the Bible and who is still with us today in wisdom, love, and power. We are caught up in the same human struggle against the caprice of nature, the evil in persons and institutions, the prevailing outcomes of accumulated human failure, and our atavistic drag and moral indifference that is often referred to as "original sin."

One may be disappointed to find that there is no "systematic" theology in the Bible, unless one can say that in Paul's epistles to the Romans, Colossians, and Galatians there is presented a kind of apologia. And yet these letters are dated and are directed at special ad hoc situations. What is found in the Bible is a self-disclosure of God, a revelation that breaks into history and into the lives of people in the context of their social arrangements.

God's Self-disclosure

The record of the self-disclosure of God in the Bible begins at the level of command and obedience, authority and fear, rewards and punishments, a powerful, unbending deity to whom one has very limited access. But as the centuries roll on and as humans ascend in their grasp of spiritual reality, this self-disclosure is more complete. Isaiah finds God ever so much closer in the Temple when King Uzziah dies, Jeremiah's knowledge of God takes us to another plateau from which we see God more clearly, and Ezekiel's vision brings God even nearer. Finally, in the pages of the New Testament, we find God in the face of Jesus Christ, at the fullness of time. Now we see God as a good shepherd, who shows more concern for the one sheep gone astray than for the ninety-nine still in the fold.

When I was a boy the day came when my daddy told me that he forgot to get my shoes out of the repair shop, with my new heavy, steel heel plates on them. I had believed that my daddy could not forget. He was a tower of authority and efficiency, a daddy without flaw. Later in my youth we played ball together and chased around on the beach. Daddy was getting more and more real to me. At his sister's funeral I saw him cry for the first time, and he became more real than ever. As the years unfolded, with the normal frequency of tragedy, success, failure, and triumph in the family, I learned to relate more and more to the resonance of his soul. My fullest appreciation of my daddy did not come until the day I became a father too, and my own receiving apparatus was ready to take it all in. When I became a father, and a grandfather as he was slowing down, and as the shadows of the evening of his days deepened, we could talk about God's mercy and love eyeball to eyeball, and talk about heaven with hushed seriousness and solemn certitude. This was yet another degree of fatherhood, richer yet than any earlier experience.

The knowledge of God that comes to us from the study of the Bible was not thrust at humankind before we were ready. There was a tedious struggle through centuries of the dim and partial spiritual discernment of the Hebrew judges, kings, prophets, and patriarchs, before the dust settled down, the dark clouds floated slowly past, and the radiance of God's fullness appeared in our Savior, Jesus Christ.

The wonder is not so much how slowly the human mind did grasp God's self-disclosure, but how patient and loving God was to bring humankind along, and how incomprehensible it is that this Divine Mind that brought worlds into being, and that continues to regulate infinite cosmic processes, would be caring enough to wait behind Mount Horeb for a young fugitive shepherd to come by with his father-in-law's sheep, and would send an encouraging word to those arid spirits by the rivers of Babylon through the prophet Ezekiel, and would overtake a fanatic like Saul of Tarsus and divert his kinetic zeal from the murder of believers to the promulgation of Christ's redeeming grace. This vision of God makes the Bible more explosive than nuclear power and more revolutionary than space flight! The story began with the human race wandering around the Tigris-Euphrates valley, and from that desert dryness of Mesopotamia it followed them on the slow trek toward an understanding of the dignity and worth of all persons. It led to a knowledge of a just God who created us for genuine community, an awareness of the zenith of human goodness in Jesus of Galilee, the experience of the guidance of the Holy Spirit, and the awareness of eternal life that begins now and is made more complete in God's presence when this earthly tabernacle is dissolved. The Bible provides the preacher with a moral and spiritual orientation toward life and persons in our communities.

The understanding of God among the early Hebrews may trouble some because today we look at God through the lenses of the Christian gospel. If one is to use the Bible as a resource for coping with community concerns, it is the God we see in Christ that guides us. As we look for God's guidance in responding to today's issues, we focus upon the requirements of the kingdom that Jesus set before us. Therefore, the regnancy of God is more than a command-obey relationship. We do not wait for orders to be flashed across the sky in bolts of lightning; we engage in prayer and reflection upon Christ's teachings and example, and act with the assurance of the presence of our God in all that we do.

The significant fact is that somewhere along the way, in the early stages of the human enterprise, it was discovered that while we shared a great deal with other created animal life—heart, liver, kidneys, brain, memory, and nervous system—we were nevertheless a quantum leap ahead of them all and "made a little lower than the angels and crowned with glory and honor." We ate, drank, reproduced, and died like the camels, the oxen, the sheep, and the goats, but we also built altars, wrote poems, played music on reeds, and made rhythm on sheets of metal; we organized extensive tribal and family systems, educated our young, and prayed to a God who was unseen and untouched. The Bible amplifies this theme and carries it on to its summit in the gospels.

Without this Bible-based consciousness of God in our midst, it would not really matter to us whether we care for the losers in our society, whether we feed the hungry, regard the basic humanity of prisoners, provide adequate foster care for unparented children, seek harmonious relations among different ethnic groups, preserve the natural ecosystem for the next generation, provide the finest educational experience for our children, or lift the aspiration of the people from mere survival and instinctive behavior to the call to the kingdom of God.

But because we are rehearsed in the Bible narratives, poetry, songs, parables, and events, we are God-centered and we do care. As we stand in the mire of today's challenges, our strength and our direction come from what we remember about Isaac redigging the wells that his father Abraham had dug, Hannah pledging to lend young Samuel to the Lord for all the days of his life, Daniel praying with his face set toward Jerusalem, Nehemiah walking through the quiet dark streets and the rubble of the Holy City before beginning to rebuild the walls, Esther going before the king and risking her life for her people, Jesus praying in the garden of Gethsemane until he sweat blood, and Paul and Silas singing all night in a Philippian jail until the jailer believed and testified.

When one's mind is saturated with the Bible, when one's life is lifted Godward, all other persons nearby feel the tug on their lives. The surrounding community and all its institutions are affected when enough people have such a worldview and such an estimation of the purposes of our days on earth. We transcend our earthbound biological and social definitions and become citizens of the eternal kingdom of God in the midst of time.

With such a grounding in the scriptures, we approach the issues confronting us in our communities spiritually prepared, poised for serious service, edified and consecrated with a mind oriented toward the things that pertain to God's kingdom on earth. We approach these issues with hope also, because of the divine initiative that we find in the Bible. The Bible declares from beginning to end that our sojourn on the earth is overarched with the abiding presence of a caring and a merciful God, whose self-disclosure is made through the veil of human experience, but fully in the face of Jesus Christ.

From External Moral Demands to Internal Moral Control

The ultimate moral control is from within. If our communities are troubled with human failure, a breakdown in moral behavior, a loss of restraint and control, the corrective lies not in more laws, bigger jails, and capital punishment. These are punitive reactions, and in the face of them the breakdown grows and continues. The trouble lies not with external legalism, from without, but with moral restraint, from within.

The moral guidance from the Bible began with the Commandments and the apodictic demands of God on the leaders of the Hebrew tribes. As time passed, and as spiritual maturity developed, this moral direction moved from external to internal restraint: from the authority/fear relationship to the loving parent/obedient child relationship. The moral monitor becomes a spiritual experience within us rather than the fear of punishment from beyond.

In the Sermon on the Mount, Jesus makes this transition clear:

> Ye have heard that it was said by them of old time, Thou shalt not kill; and whosoever shall kill shall be in danger of the judgment: But I say unto you, That whosoever is angry with his brother without a cause shall be in danger of the judgment. (Matthew 5:21)

Throughout this centerpiece of Jesus' teaching, there is an appeal to let one's conduct flow from within, from a desire and motivation that are authentically one's very own, not simply from an outward compliance to expectations and commands. Indeed, this approach did not cancel the requirements of the law, it exceeded them by calling for behavior more genuine, more sincere, more volitional, coming from within.

As Christians we know this transition does not take place by gritting our teeth, clenching our fists, and stomping our feet. We have no power to convert this vessel of clay into an instrument of God's grace. This moral restraint comes from God.

In the Old Testament the controlling power was the Spirit of God. Through divine intuition God spoke to the prophets of old. Later, this restraint was provided by the immediate leadership of Jesus Christ; after the Resurrection, the empowerment of the Holy Spirit sufficed.

This experience of inner moral restraint was introduced to many of us through our families, our teachers, our neighbors, choir leaders, and pastors. We were led into it by caring people. My own father never *sent* me to Sunday school. He carried me. He was there with me. On the other hand, our consciences *could* have been nurtured by the ethics, the rules, the taboos, and the sanctions of our peers in school and in the streets. The conscience is furnished in many ways, depending upon the influences, the loyalties, and the belief system to which we subscribe. If one is prepared by a knowledge of the historical Jesus, his teachings and his example, and believes in him as God's son and our Savior, and surrenders his or her life in submission to God's will, and receives God's Spirit, he or she becomes a new creation. The old loyalties are supplanted by the fruits of the Spirit. This is what Paul meant when he said, "I am crucified with Christ; nevertheless I live, yet not I, but Christ liveth in me: and the life which I now live in the flesh I live by the faith of the Son of God, who loved me, and gave himself for me" (Gal. 2:20).

So the Spirit of Christ in us does for us what no legalism from without could ever do. It equips us with a new ego, a new personhood, a new self. And, there is distinct moral content to this new self; "the fruit of the Spirit is love, joy, peace, longsuffering, gentleness, goodness, faith, meekness, temperance" (Gal. 5:22–23). Now we see why someone called the Epistle to the Galatians the Magna Carta of the Christian faith. It gets to the heart of the whole matter.

This understanding of Christian experience, a new life that manifests itself in love and service, prevents that awful dichotomy whereby some Christians emphasize social action and neglect evangelism and others emphasize evangelism and neglect social action. If we study the teachings of Jesus and Paul we find that such a bifurcation of Christian experience is plainly wrong and unwarranted. Social action to relieve suffering and to correct injustice is the other side of the coin that calls for repentance, belief, confession, surrender, and the indwelling of the Holy Spirit. Christian life is one complete experience.

Nothing is more crucial to our communities than this. A changed society calls for changed persons. A child of God does not want to live on drugs, does not want to beg rather than work, to sell the body into prostitution, to pollute the mind with filthy movies, to waste money on alcohol, to abandon or abuse helpless children, to accept crooks and thieves as representatives, or to waste educational opportunity.

The child of God wants to honor God with a life of beauty and service, commitment and sacrifice, and to cause redeeming love to be manifested in personal relations as well as in social and public affairs. Personal and social salvation are one, but whereas the law has its place and function to compel minimal conformity, the lively and dynamic movement toward the kingdom of God is propelled from within, from a heart possessed by the love of God.

The Cultivation of a Sense of Community

One of the continuing problems facing us is the estrangement of groups from one another in our pluralistic society. The movement in the Bible from tribalism to community in Christ is therefore highly significant for us.

Our geographic community boundaries are only one dimension of an understanding of community. We may know very well where our physical communities begin and end, defined by their architectural homogeneity, economic status, and traffic patterns, but such elements do not create real community among persons. Do two community members pass each other like ships in the night, or are they aware of each other? Are there common needs and concerns they should address together? Are there any values they share that would enhance the quality of life in the neighborhood?

Christians have much to share because of the unique community that we claim in Christ. Other forms of togetherness are transcended insofar as this community in Christ finds its basis at the deepest and most profound levels of our existence. We are together in Christ because we share the knowledge of God that was revealed in Jesus, we are centered morally on the standards that Jesus exemplified, we are empowered by the Holy Spirit whose presence was invoked in our behalf, we live in that immortality *now* to which Jesus has inducted us, our sins are forgiven by virtue of Jesus' persistence, even unto the cross, and our hope is sustained by his risen Spirit that goes before us in triumph over sin, Satan, and the grave. All of this binds us together in Christian community.

Our local challenge is to generate such a thrust toward this level of community that the negative undertow of racial and ethnic strife will dissipate itself.

The Bible bears witness to this movement toward inclusivism. From the time when the ancestors of the Israelites first migrated into Palestine to the sixth century B.C., from Abraham to the prophet whose message begins at Isaiah 40, there is a movement from a closed ethnocentricity to a larger, deeper awareness of God's total human family.

The self-disclosure of God began at a given place and time, among a given people. It had to start somewhere, but as time passed and moral and spiritual maturity ripened, it became necessary, although difficult, for the prophets to make clear that God was God of all humanity, one God with one morality, one righteousness covering all people.

Elijah became so exhausted in his defense of Jehovah that he lapsed into moments of deep resignation and cried out in anguish, begging to die. His crusade for the one true God against Ahab and Jezebel found him making paths through strange woodlands, hiding in quiet places where birds were safe and unafraid, drinking water from virgin streams with his cupped hands, and sleeping in caves. This isolation was self-imposed that he might be free to fight for the idea of one God over all humanity.

Jeremiah, the servant of God who learned to live in that abyss between the idolatry of his people and the jealousy of a righteous God, was put into Pashur's stocks for declaring that Israel had no moral exemptions.

Amos and Micah lifted the universal principle of justice above ritual and sacrifice, above tribal taboos and proscriptions, above traditions and genetic blood lines, and made it the highest claim on God's people.

The sixth century saw a great change in the lives of the Jewish people. Two generations of Jews were forced to survive as exiles in Babylon under King Nebuchadnezzar and wait for their deliverance by Cyrus the Great. In all of this they saw the hand of God. They cried that they could not sing the songs of Zion in a strange land, but Isaiah told them to wait on the Lord and they would rise up as on eagles' wings; and Ezekiel said he had seen their valley of dry bones in a vision and that the bones had all reassembled and marched like a mighty army.

They survived, but when they returned to Jerusalem, with Ezra and Nehemiah leading the rebuilding of both the walls of the city and the morale of the people, they were called to a larger view of their role in the world. They were no longer to revert to a closed religious community, but to "lengthen their cords and strengthen their stakes." Isaiah said, "It is a light thing that thou shouldest be my servant to raise up the tribes of Jacob, and to restore the preserved of Israel: I will also give thee for a light to the Gentiles, that thou mayest be my salvation unto the end of the earth" (Isa. 49:6). They found themselves called to a ministry and a prophetic service beyond their own tribes.

Perhaps the most dramatic appeals to inclusiveness came to them from the writers of Ruth and Jonah. The Book of Ruth presents Naomi, an Israelite mother-in-law, with a Moabite daughter-in-law, a young woman of a separate group and another religion. Moabites were not accepted by Israelites. Naomi's husband and two sons had died in Moab, and as she left the land of Moab to journey home to Israel she advised her two daughters-in-law to remain in their own land. One did, but the other, Ruth, persisted in following her mother-in-law to Israel.

As the story unfolds, Ruth went with Naomi, saying, "Entreat me not to leave thee, or to return from following after thee: for whither thou goest, I will go; and where thou lodgest, I will lodge: thy people shall be my people, and thy God my God" (Ruth 1:16).

The story now challenges centuries of tradition, legalism, and exclusiveness. Ruth, the Moabite, marries an Israelite named Boaz. From this union descends David, Israel's most illustrious king—with a Moabite great-grandmother!—and later Joseph, the husband of Mary, the mother of Jesus Christ. Clearly, when this writer went to the extent of showing that David descended from a Moabite, it was intended to shatter the notion that one had to be of a particular blood line to please God. The whole human family had one true God.

Jonah was written by another inspired writer, who made the same point. God commanded Jonah to go and preach to the Ninevites, those oppressors! Jonah refused; it took three days in the whale to convince Jonah that God cared for Ninevites as much as for Israelites. The circle is widening. Tribalism is receding and a broader community of believers is coming into focus. The inclusive Spirit of God is moving.

When John preached at the Jordan of the advent of the kingdom of God, some came announcing that they were sons of Abraham. John declared that it did not matter whose sons they were. He said that God could make sons of Abraham out of stones. What did matter was a new basis of community, repentance from sin and acceptance of the regnancy of God.

Jesus made it clear when he received Samaritans, Romans, Greeks, Phoenicians, thieves, tax collectors, lepers, Roman soldiers, harlots, wine bibbers, and sinners into his fellowship, saying, "Whosoever will let him come." God's reach in Jesus Christ probed all the thin barriers of race, class, sex, and moral standing.

Paul continued declaring that in Christ we had a liberty that transcended tribe and clan and made us all new creations. And the rapturous vision of John on Patmos was that of a multitude that no one could number, of every race and tongue, crying glory and honor to the Lamb who sat upon the throne of God.

The witness of the Bible is unquestioned: God intended that we should be one family, bound together by our faithfulness in the blessed community. The Bible overflows with messages on this theme. This is the basis of our concern about the estrangement and alienation that afflict our communities.

The Role and Status of Women and Children

The foundation of any society is the inescapable biological fact of the family. At the base of the human family is the need of the human infant for protection and care while the superior and complicated nervous system, with all its potential for genius or destruction, is maturing. Whenever these facts are ignored or treated lightly, the consequences have been disastrous. Therefore, the message of the Bible about women and children is crucial.

There is no more pressing issue in our communities today than the family and the rearing of children. The preacher finds the largest segment of time devoted to problems and challenges emanating from the abuse of the privilege that God has given to us to reproduce.

In the earliest agrarian economic systems, before there was sophisticated farming equipment, all able hands were needed for production. Consequently, the number of wives and children became part of the inventory of the total operation. It was often difficult to distinguish between the way in which the animals were treated and the treatment accorded the women. In such a situation women accepted a role more as object than as person. In Genesis 16:2–4, the barren Sarah offers her maid, Hagar, to her husband, Abraham. He accepts and by this Egyptian maid a son, Ishmael, is born.

In 2 Samuel 3:2–5 we read that David had six sons while at Hebron, each by a different mother. Later, Solomon was born to David by Uriah's wife, Bathsheba. By today's standards this is another world and by the standards of Jesus this is morally primitive. In 1 Kings 11:1–3 we read that Solomon "loved many strange women . . . the daughter of Pharaoh . . . women of the Moabites, Ammonites, Edomites,

Zidonians, and Hittites." He had seven hundred wives
and three hundred concubines. Then he went after the
goddess of the Zidonians, Milcom. He collected
women!

The history of the treatment of women is very uneven, but in the gospels the entire atmosphere is radi-
cally different from that in the days of Abraham,
David, and Solomon. Jesus showed great empathy
with the woman who was about to be stoned to death
for adultery in John 8:3–11. The encounter closes as
he challenges her accusers and says to her, "Neither
do I condemn thee: go, and sin no more." Likewise,
in John 4:7–30 we find one of the most beautiful examples of Jesus' compassion in his conversation with the
Samaritan woman at the well at Sychar, who has already been married five times and is living unmarried
with the sixth man. Jesus looked upon these women as
victims of male caprice and abuse, not as property.

The gospels further reflect the love and concern
that Jesus held for children. Perhaps the most eman-
cipating word he gave was when he admonished his
followers to have faith and humility as pure and as
trusting as a child's. And then came the strongest declaration, in Matthew 18:5–6:

> And whoso shall receive one such little child in my
> name receiveth me. But whoso shall offend one of
> these little ones which believe in me, it were better for
> him that a millstone were hanged about his neck, and
> that he were drowned in the depth of the sea.

The good news is laden with moral content. We are
saved *from* sin but we are also saved *to* a higher standard of behavior, manifested most especially in this
basic human relationship, the treatment of women
and children.

The witness of the Bible is especially strong because in its early stages it reflects the crude and heartless abuse of women as mere objects of the whim of males. Consider that in order for Esther to be appropriately prepared to spend her one night with the king she had to be treated with myrrh and other perfumes for twelve months. But by the time the Bible has finished exposing this awful treatment of women to the love of God, it is closing with the resounding refrain, "There is neither male nor female: for ye are all one in Christ Jesus" (Gal. 3:28).

Our concern today for equal opportunity for women, adequate education and care for children, an enlightened juvenile crime program, support for dependent children, ridding our streets and schools of drugs, and fair divorce, insurance, and estate laws, follows the witness of the Bible at its sublime height in the teaching and example of Jesus Christ.

From a Life of Abundance to the Abundant Life

At the source of much of our moral concern is the fact that our generation seems to be hypnotized by materialism and consumerism. Our appetites are whetted by our obsession with a growth economy, sustained by incessant advertising. Our understanding of adequacy is luxury, and success is therefore ceaseless acquisition. Satisfaction becomes tantamount to wealth and the life of abundance.

This quest to acquire the tokens of material success fuels such outcomes as bribery in high places, corporations cheating on defense contracts, physicians padding Medicaid bills, police selling protection to crime syndicates, and young street criminals snatching necklaces and pocketbooks, selling crack, and entering prostitution. The craving is endemic; we blindly associate abundance with the good life.

The Bible brings a different perspective to us. True, it starts out equating wealth with the good life. Recall how Abraham, Isaac, Jacob, and Joseph were all blessed with herds of cattle, flocks of sheep, processions of camels loaded with goods, and countless servants and concubines.

In Deuteronomy 8:12–13 the signs of God's goodness and approval are eating to the full, living in goodly houses, and having one's flocks and other possessions multiply. The instruction to tithe in Malachi 3:10 is accompanied by a promise that the faithful will see the windows of heaven opened and blessings poured out so bountifully that there will not be space to receive them. Give your tithes and offerings; prepare for the bounties of heaven!

In the Book of Proverbs, 3:9–10, we are admonished to honor the Lord with our substance, and in return our barns will be filled and our presses bursting with new wine.

Job was a rich man who was tested by the loss of everything. His body even was covered with sores. And as a reward for his unfeigned faith, all of his wealth was restored. In Job 42:12 we read, "So the LORD blessed the latter end of Job more than his beginning: for he had fourteen thousand sheep, and six thousand camels, and a thousand yoke of oxen, and a thousand she asses."

But this understanding of the good life is challenged by the authors of the Book of Daniel and the Book of Esther. In Daniel we find that faithfulness to God is given the highest priority. Daniel and the three Hebrew young men are offered a chance for material comfort in the king's palace but they reject that for the lions' den and the fiery furnace in order to be faithful to God.

Esther was the Persian queen, destined to live in luxury as long as she concealed her background and her religion. But Esther's cousin Mordecai convinced her that her people were suffering while she enjoyed the luxury of the king's palace. She had a choice either to go to the king in her people's behalf, and risk condemnation and death, or to continue to hide her racial and religious identity and remain comfortable. She takes the risk. In so doing she elevates the value of honor, of courage, of faithfulness to God above that of wealth and personal luxury.

A maturing understanding of God's will reveals that while the acquisition of wealth might be the outcome of prudence and hard work, such wealth is not the total fulfillment of life's purpose. Getting and having are not the same as becoming pleasing in God's sight.

The life of Christ calls us to a more complete understanding of the secondary place that should be assigned to the life of abundance of material goods. First place is given to the abundant life, rich in physical well-being, concern for others, love and reverence toward God, moral sincerity and transparency, humility, service, and a transcending faithfulness in the kingdom of God.

In fact Jesus was suspicious of the rich. A rich young ruler came to him asking what he needed to do to inherit eternal life. It was agreed that one should keep the Ten Commandments. When the young man boasted that he had kept all the commandments, Jesus raised the standard to a higher level of perfection, calling upon him to give all he had to the poor.

Jesus himself lived a life of detachment from concern for material well-being. Whatever he intended

for us mortals to do, it was surely something other
than getting rich. His own simplicity and inner security put us to shame with our childish adoration of the
life of abundance.

Jesus reversed the Old Testament image of the life
of abundance as a sign of God's favor, and in its place
he said, in John 10:10, "I am come that they might
have life, and that they might have it more abun-
dantly." This abundant life was within, the joy of a new
fellowship with God, the release from sin, the peace of
soul that Christ affords, and the blessed hope of eternal life. His counsel (in Matthew 6:19–21) was:

> Lay not up for yourselves treasures upon earth, where
> moth and rust doth corrupt, and where thieves break
> through and steal: But lay up for yourselves treasures
> in heaven, where neither moth nor rust doth corrupt,
> and where thieves do not break through nor steal: For
> where your treasure is, there will your heart be also.

This teaching may seem irrelevant to community
concerns, but it lies at the center of such issues. The
blatant materialism of our society is making life cheap
and destroying purpose and meaning for us. We are
without aim and purpose except making and getting
money. This reduces life for all of us to a vulgar competitiveness so that the enhancement of the quality of
life for all is secondary.

We are called to turn our loyalties to those endeav-
ors that lift us above instinctive and survival behavior
to something more worthy of our Creator and the
crowning achievement of creation.

4

Trusting the Voice
That Comes from Within

His word was in mine heart as a burning fire shut up in
my bones, and I was weary with forbearing, and I could
not stay.
—Jeremiah 20:9

When we face the crises and concerns in our communities, we need to prepare ourselves through
prayer and reflection, through Bible study and medita-
tion, to hear the word that God may speak to us to
guide us over the difficult terrain ahead.

From the depths of our souls there comes to us
every now and then an intuitive insight, a word of
wisdom, a word of comfort, a word of courage, a word
of caution, a word of peace. There is a part of us that
does not live by bread and water but by every word
that proceeds out of the mouth of God. All of us have
had the experience at some time or other that we are
being directed from within, that there is within us
something more than physical organs—a spiritual part
of our being that guides and directs our lives.

Throughout the Bible we find one person after another reporting that the Lord has spoken to her or to

him, not in words that others can hear but from within, through the depths of the soul. God has used this intuitive capacity to call a prophet from Tekoa to sound the trumpet for justice, to send John to the Jordan to herald a new kingdom, and to stop Paul on the Damascus road and reverse the course of his life. But one has to be extremely careful that he or she does not mistake private prejudices for the voice of God.

Can We Trust Our Intuition?

During the late 1950s when the issue of desegregation was foremost in public debate, there were those who came forth with opinions in favor of continued segregation that they attributed to a "voice" from within. During those debates one pastor discovered some minutes of a meeting in 1883 of his small congregation in rural Virginia. They recorded the testimony of a white member who had prayed over the fact that blacks and whites were worshiping together as members of the same church. He claimed that the Lord "told" him it was wrong. Consequently, that little church split and one group created a new black church. Apparently the Lord "told" the same thing to several others, because during that period many congregations separated from their black members. Obviously, this "voice" was the culture and the dominant social mores challenging the innocent practice of churches in allowing blacks and whites to worship together.

Whereas it is true that we are equipped for intuitive knowledge and insight, and the testimony of countless prophets and saints has been that they, like Elijah, have all heard a still, small voice, nevertheless we are human and very fallible. Often in the name of God slave dealers prayed for safe passage, warriors asked blessings on their swords and chariots, and preachers fleeced unsuspecting and devoted followers.

We are confronted daily with a wide range of issues, and it would be wonderful if we could be sure of what is being said to us from within. As serious Christians, impelled by the love of Christ, we go to our place of prayer and wait for guidance and direction. When some word comes, how do we know that God is speaking and not the voice of the prevailing TV preacher, or the latest pamphlet that came in the mail, or what the congressional representative advocates, or what the local newspaper stands for?

This problem is all the more serious for the preacher who addresses the people on community concerns. Most of these concerns have already divided the community, pro and con, and often the church is also divided. There are conflicting answers to the question of how much government initiative in monitoring social outcomes is enough, how much one generation is responsible for correcting the abuses and injustices of previous generations, how much the middle class should be asked to pay to assist those who are marginal, how far society can go in making up for the failures of parents, what the poor deserve and when they have been given enough, who is responsible for the health care of the indigent, what is the best thing to do with street criminals, how one deals with white-collar crime, who is responsible for the aesthetic and recreational opportunities of a community, how high taxes should be.

On the other hand, communities are sometimes so monolithic that there is little problem in getting agreement on any of these issues. Such unanimity is based on class rigidities, vested interests, and social distance. Many have inherited their social means and protect them by associating only with those who share the same style of life. If such persons ever hear a still, small voice, it will probably say something familiar and palatable.

Many preachers who are partisans on these questions find it difficult to find sanction in their hearts for any other position. And, their still, small voice generally agrees!

We are all so conditioned by our early exposures—childhood influences, the ideals of our parents, the taboos of the neighborhood, the boundaries of our circle of approved people, the jokes we heard, the rhymes we learned, the stories we listened to, the television we watched—that by the time we reach adulthood the whole package of values is wrapped and sealed. Our basic personhood is set; our ego has negotiated its position. And mostly we look, then, for validation and approval, acceptance and inclusion. Those voices that speak to us on another wavelength are often rejected and tuned out. But we turn up the volume for those who resonate with our values and beliefs, who sound the way we want them to sound.

We do this in the choices we make in our personal lives too—how we spend our money, how we use our time, how we relate to friends, wives, and children, what we call acceptable standards for personal conduct. We listen for what we want to hear. How much more is this true with community concerns! We hear those voices that leave the status quo undisturbed; we hear the messages that speak comfortably to our own social class; we hear the voices that whisper peace when it is time for agitation, protest, and indignation. We like to hear those familiar ideas that require hardly any change at all.

For example, many preachers have prayed about the ordination of women and have heard no answer but the one they began with. Even the apostle Paul found

it difficult to escape the influence of his youth as a
rabbinical student. In 1 Corinthians 7:25, Paul said,
"Now concerning virgins I have no commandment of
the Lord." In other words, God was silent on this
topic. But Paul went on anyway: "Yet I give my judgment, as one that hath obtained mercy of the Lord to
be faithful." Then he presented *his* views on marriage,
which reflected *his* upbringing as a Hebrew of the
Hebrews, of the tribe of Benjamin and a Pharisee;
blameless in matters of the Law.

So where he had no clear word from God he proceeded on his own, in the light of his own background.
The culture we inherit is a strong force. We need to
be careful that we do not equate our own cultural
habits with the voice of God.

One of the most serious tasks we face is learning to
distinguish the voice of God from our own preoccupa-
tions and loyalties. Clearly, we need some way to test
the voices we hear. Something may be churning in us,
like the word that burned in Jeremiah, but how do we
test these voices from within? Some may be no more
than the echo of an old, hoary prejudice that was conceived in inequity and born in consuming hate and
bigotry; some may be our own frustrated ambitions
and ego fantasies rattling around; some may be our
naïve and ill-founded expectations, personal whims
waiting for substance and validity and hurried along in
our minds in the form of a misty dream.

It will be a great temptation for us to ask God to
agree with our position on every community concern
rather than earnestly to seek God's guidance. When
Martin Luther King, Jr., went to the pastorate of the
Dexter Avenue Baptist Church in Montgomery, he
followed an intellectual giant, Dr. Vernon Johns. And
King would say to his friends repeatedly that it was his
hope to become an intellectual giant like Johns, or like

Benjamin E. Mays, Howard Thurman, or Mordecai
Johnson. In many ways he did, but he followed a different course altogether. When Rosa Parks was ar-
rested for refusing to follow the Jim Crow seating on
the bus, new leadership was called for among the black
community in Montgomery. King was new in town but
exceedingly well prepared. Rather than becoming
simply an intellectual pulpiteer, he was that and more;
he was killed while working with the garbagemen of
Memphis for improved work benefits. The voice of
God prevailed.

Intuition and the World of Facts

As we seek God's guidance and listen for the voice
from within while addressing community concerns,
what are the tests that will enable us to trust as authen-
tic the voice from within? The first test is to ask if what
is said corresponds to the facts already in hand. After
all, God would not lie. Religion cannot stake its claims
on falsehoods, silly untruths, or misinformation.
Surely God has power to transcend the natural order
and perform miracles, but God also created the world
described and expressed by our logic, mathematics,
chemistry, physics, music, medicine, geography, and
astronomy. Would God tell me something that vio-
lates plain facts and that flies in the face of logic?

One day I happened to see a healing service on
television. I believe that God can and does heal. But
I believe that this matter is exploited for money also.
This popular program proclaimed that God was healing backs on that day. It sounded like a sale at the
supermarket: Backs today! I watched the screen in
disbelief. And then the preacher put his hand on his
lower back, on the right side, and said, "He is working
right here, right now." He shouted out over the air, "If

anyone has a pain right here, right now, God is healing this part now!" Well, I doubt that God told him any such thing. It defies everything I know about God's creation and how God operates.

The voice you hear giving you guidance ought to deal in facts. God is not the author of ignorance and lies. When we speak for God, what we are saying ought to rest on facts. It ought to be responsible. It ought to connect with the whole truth.

Granted, now, God is active and involved in creation, in history, and in the affairs of humankind. Granted, further, God has equipped us with intuitive capacity—all of us, not only the Quakers and the mystics. Granted also that praying preachers may commune with God and hear the still, small voice. Before she or he acts on that message, there is a need to be humble enough, concerned enough, honest enough, and responsible enough to subject that revelation to the wider forum of relevant and known facts.

If God has laid it on a pastor to speak out on prison reform, denouncing the revolving-door system that takes in offenders, educates them in all of the new ways of committing crimes without getting caught, and then returns them to the streets, that pastor had better check the data. How much actual recidivism is there? How many inmates really do have former convictions? This information gives the sermon the authenticity that it needs. There is nothing so admirable as honesty and straightforwardness, even in the pulpit!

And by the way, when we apply this test of checking the facts, our petty divisions diminish, we understand each other more clearly, we are better able to come together, and we can maintain some continuity and impact because we are communicating with each other and not speaking in unknown tongues. If our religious insights and experiences are a little more accountable to empirical truth, we will have more basis for mutual understanding.

Intuition and the Witness of the Bible

Looking further, when we are testing whether the voice that speaks is the voice of God, I suggest we consult that sacred library that has been with us for so long, the sixty-six books of the Bible. If I want to know if what I hear sounds like the voice of God, I may ask, Does it sound like what any of the great spiritual pioneers might have said?

Does it sound like Isaiah saying, "The Spirit of the Lord GOD is upon me; because the LORD hath anointed me to preach good tidings unto the meek"?

Does it sound like the psalmist saying, "Who shall ascend into the hill of the LORD? Or who shall stand in his holy place? He that hath clean hands, and a pure heart"?

Does it sound like Micah saying, "What doth the LORD require of thee, but to do justly, and to love mercy, and to walk humbly with thy God"?

Does it sound like Paul saying, "And though I give my body to be burned, and have not charity, it profiteth me nothing"?

Whenever the Bible reaches these majestic crescendos, when all the stops are wide open, it is talking not about private, personal, egocentric concerns. It is talking about lofty and sublime themes, and usually about our relations with others.

So if a voice has spoken to you, listen for how it resonates with the great themes that keep recurring in the scriptures.

Obviously, there will not be any direct references in the Bible to public school issues, teenage pregnancies, or crack, the new and deadly street drug. And if one chooses to go "proof-texting," snatching phrases out of their context, or if the Bible is looked upon as a specifications manual for living in urban America, one will not find the guidance needed. Each book of the Bible has its own audience, date, and destination. As we study what God inspired the writers to record about a given people at a given time in relationship to God, it informs us, prepares us, and deepens our knowledge of God. Moreover, we read the Bible through Christian lenses, with the mind of Christ. His teachings and his example become the canon by which we understand the high points, and the low, in God's dealings with people in the Bible.

Paul was influenced by the prevailing Roman customs on slavery, the treatment of women, and subservience to Caesar. Through the eyes of Jesus I see things differently, but I understand Paul. God was in Christ, and I measure Leviticus, Ruth, 1 and 2 Kings, Esther, and Micah by the yardstick of Jesus. This standard helps us in understanding some of the early stages of moral development, such as those children Abraham had by his concubines (Gen. 25:6). The killings in Judges, Samuel, Kings, and Chronicles fall on a scale far beneath Jesus, and the Song of Solomon hardly meets the standard of the mind of Christ. In the first chapter there is a color bias!

When we look at the Bible through the lenses of Christ, we find a wealth of moral and spiritual experience recorded there that covers a variety of human needs and will surely enable us to test some of our own spiritual experience. Consider the stories of Moses and Aaron, Ruth and Naomi, Mordecai and Esther, Joseph and his brothers, Nehemiah and the people, Paul and Mark. It is by these peaks of the Bible that one tests the voice that is speaking from within. Does

what we hear sound like anything God said to the
towering personalities of the Bible? The community
concerns that we face have some unique details, but
they have in common those basic elements of human
nature that have beset humans from the beginning.

Intuition and the Mind of Christ

Finally, when the voice speaks, ask if it sounds like
anything Jesus would say. The revelation of God in
Christ stands before us as the rule, the canon, the
yardstick by which we measure our lives. Now, if God
was in Christ, wouldn't the voice of God speaking to
you, guiding you, directing you, sound like Jesus?
While the inner voice on a given issue may resemble
the Chamber of Commerce, or the Democratic Party,
or the League of Women Voters, or the *Christian Century*, or William F. Buckley, or the *New Republic*, that
is incidental. Does it sound like Jesus?

The compassion of Christ will lead us into creative
responses to community concerns. A person with
AIDS is not beyond range of the love of Christ. The
street people, the bag women, the homeless in our
cities are very close to the kinds of people Jesus served
in his earthly ministry. If God is calling us, what the
message says will sound like something Jesus might
say also.

We are now facing the embarrassment of seeing
persons who claim to be "born-again Christians"
identifying themselves with militarism and unbridled
super patriotism, rejecting the poor, calling for the
reversal of civil rights gains, and opposing federal activity that improves life chances for the poor. They
speak loudly of being born again and of being led by
the Holy Spirit. And yet, so much of what they stand

for is alien to the gospel and the good news of God. They need badly to read Matthew 25 again and then ask if the voice within is really the voice of God.

On a Sunday in church, a friend who is a dentist noticed one choir member in particular. Her voice had been heard there for thirty-five years. But she was very self-conscious in her declining years because her teeth were decayed and she could not afford dental work. While the preacher was preaching and the chants and anthems and hymns rang forth in unbroken praise, something spoke to him in that service.

The next day he called her to come in, took X-rays, made preliminary probings around the remaining teeth, and set a date to extract them all and take a mold for brand-new plates. She protested to him that she was broke, and he told her that "something" told him to do this for her. She cried—from shock and joy and thanksgiving.

She hasn't stopped telling people yet that she wonders what that "something" was that spoke to him. Well, we all know who it was. It was the Lord speaking. And it sounded just like Jesus.

The voice of God in Christ will speak to us on community concerns. It will bring a word of charity, a word of forgiveness and reconciliation, a word of love and renewal, a word of power and strength. It will speak to those persons and conditions that Jesus dealt with; it will speak of the sick and the helpless, of the blind and the lame, the lepers, the harlots, the wine bibbers, the children, the widows, and those farthest out. This voice will not speak of denying food to the hungry in favor of death-dealing bombs; it will not speak of withholding benefits from children who did not ask to be born; it will not speak of embarrassing the elderly by making beggars of them; it will not speak of allowing

mentally incompetent street people to sleep in the
snow. The voice that speaks of hatred and divisiveness
is not the voice of God.

The good news of the gospel has so much to say on
community concerns. Our religion is a moral religion.
It does not provide ecstasy and deliverance without
moral accountability. Jesus said that the sheep in the
judgment were the ones who cared about the least of
these, and the goats who were condemned did not (see
Matthew 25). If you have a word to proclaim in the
name of God, the content ought to square with who
Jesus was and what he did.

In a New Jersey town a man's mind snapped and he
went home and brutally killed the two small children
of his common-law wife. The story revealed that he
had had mental problems for quite some time and
should not have been caring for anyone's children. It
turned out that he had been asking for help. He had
gone to a downtown church the Sunday before to see
if someone would talk with him, and they followed the
conventional wisdom, the polite protocol, and drove
him out of their clean church. He wasn't dressed right,
didn't smell right, didn't look like the other churchgo-
ers.

"Something" told them to drive him out, but that
"something" was not Jesus. The Master says:

> Come unto me, all ye that labour and are heavy laden,
> and I will give you rest. Take my yoke upon you, and
> learn of me; for I am meek and lowly in heart: and ye
> shall find rest unto your souls. For my yoke is easy, and
> my burden is light. (Matthew 11:28–30)

Voices we can trust sound like the voice of Christ.

5

Crises and Priorities

Five times I have received at the hands of the Jews the forty lashes less one. Three times I have been beaten with rods; once I was stoned. Three times I have been ship-wrecked; a night and a day I have been adrift at sea; on frequent journeys, in danger from rivers, danger from robbers, danger from my own people, danger from Gentiles, danger in the city, danger in the wilderness, danger at sea, danger from false brethren; in toil and hardship, through many a sleepless night, in hunger and thirst, often without food, in cold and exposure. And, apart from other things, there is the daily pressure upon me of my anxiety for all the churches.
—2 Corinthians 11:24–28, RSV

Because as pastors we are called to be involved in the lives of people, we are among the first to feel the pain of violent oppression, unmitigated suffering, and long-term neglect as they erupt in episodic crises in our communities. Because of our training, experience, and sensitivity we feel pain at the closing of a neighborhood health facility, the brutal treatment of a helpless person, or an announcement of extremely low reading scores in a school serving those who need help the most. When one end of town becomes an armed camp, when poverty is so pervasive that except for dogs and cats the streets are empty in a large area, or when a crime wave has everyone buying new locks and alarm systems and many are carrying handguns and hunting knives, we choke with tension and lie awake for hours. We wonder what we can do.

Often ours are the only voices that can be trusted to speak without bias or a hidden agenda. People look to us for cool, hard facts and fair interpretations. If we go into hiding in the midst of a crisis we will be like the shepherd who runs and leaves the sheep when the wolf approaches.

In 1977 all the lights went out in New York City. Elevators stopped between floors in skyscrapers, air-conditioners were silenced and ovens turned off, food in refrigerators spoiled, traffic lights were out so driving was even more precarious, hospitals started up their feeble miniature generators, computers were stuck, televisions were silent, the red hue in the Gotham sky from the neon lights was no longer seen, and Broadway stood still. New York had ground to a halt. By the next Sunday, the glaze of shock was still on the faces of the people, and we preachers all had to respond to their loss of confidence in technology.

In 1965 New York suffered a long transit strike. Automobiles were snarled in endless traffic jams, people sold apartments and quit good jobs, nerves were on edge, all patience was spent, the poor could not get to work, the able walked miles from Brooklyn and the Bronx to Lower Manhattan, and the city's endurance was sorely tested. Again, the preachers had to speak comfortably to the people. These crises, though of great magnitude, did not involve group tensions or hatred. However, other crises that do involve group, class, or racial tensions seem to come in cycles, causing everyone to tremble, telephones to stay warm, headlines to blast, tempers to flare; and every preacher is as jumpy as a firehouse dog. That blessful tranquillity that we once knew is gone—when people stayed married, before casinos opened in Atlantic City, when blacks were living out a tacit compromise, when Vietnam was still French Indo-China, Bing Crosby and Jack Benny were on the radio, children obeyed, DeSotos were cabs and Packards were limousines, policemen rode bicycles, and the subway cost a nickel. And our sermons reflect the change. Every week there is another community crisis waiting to be addressed.

Establishing Our Preaching Priorities

One way to deal with the preaching agenda is to preach from television's eleven o'clock news, *Time,* and the morning paper, from the outcomes, failures, and results of our social maelstrom. The preacher has then no fundamental, sustained ministry of the Word. He or she is like a short-order cook on a ferryboat, keeping up with whatever is shouted out last. Crises do need a quick response, but preaching to community concerns requires also a steady diet of solid, continuous attention to certain priority issues that underlie many of the crisis issues that emerge. As with medical care, it is not enough to go to the doctor's office only when there is pain or fever. There must be annual examinations for silent destroyers like hypertension, diabetes, glaucoma, high cholesterol, obesity, alcoholism, and smoking. Regular care limits the crisis potential. People are better able to handle crises when the pastor has given attention to certain priority issues that are basic to the health and stability of the community.

Once I had an invitation from a college president who wanted to talk with me about a position at his institution. As we talked I sensed that he was feeling for words. I tried to help but suddenly he stood up and said, "Sam, I need a vice-president for *tone*—to give some tone to this place!" I hardly felt able, but I found out what he meant. Students were not studying, coaches and athletes dominated the campus from one season to another, faculty meetings were shallow and aimless, few persons were using the new and shining library, lectures by visiting scholars were poorly attended, seniors were not getting into strong graduate programs, and few alumni had achieved much after graduation. He wanted to do something fast to turn the school around and make it look and feel like a community of scholars. But he really needed to tighten up on promotion standards, bring in new leadership in instruction, enrich the mix of the freshmen and sophomore curriculum, establish a faculty exchange program, stimulate writing and research, have groups of students and faculty meeting frequently to start some campus conversation, invite provocative speakers, send students and faculty to challenging conferences, create rewards for faculty and student achievements, promote more lectures, and involve students and faculty in scheduling and planning. All these things were needed to "give some tone" to the school.

If every community had a team of preachers who kept the "tone" of the good news before the people with relevant, timely preaching, keeping Christ alive before them, letting the historical Jesus of Galilee, Judea, and Perea walk before them, and the risen Christ of the ages inspire and strengthen them, while lifting up those conditions that the good news exposes and seeks to redeem, the churches would reflect the "tone" of the good news of God.

It is one thing to keep abreast of the immediate and episodic events and concerns, but along with that the church should let the "tone" of the good news be known and felt in the community. The way to do this is for the pastor to be identified with certain priorities that are illuminated by the good news. The concerns of the community must be seen in a broader context and given the significance that the good news will assign to them.

What are some examples of community concerns that call for longer-term therapy, where quick fixes will not do, and for which there must be a constant consciousness-raising effort? There are several, but let us examine three such priority concerns.

The Priority of Eliminating Poverty Amid Plenty

A first priority in almost every place in America is meeting the needs of homeless and hungry people, and this raises a broader issue of income and available benefits. The facts are that some industries have fallen upon hard times. The people who are displaced by these failing industries, or their auxiliaries, will become economically displaced, and many of them could join the ranks of the homeless and hungry. Also, 20 million illiterate Americans are often out of work, in between jobs, and will remain so. Society is now knowledge-intensive. Lifting, hauling, baling, shucking, and packing are all mechanized processes, and no one is needed who is merely strong.

Therefore, many of the homeless and hungry are in the streets because there is no place for them in our economy. The service jobs in fast foods and the like pay so little that workers cannot meet their needs. They are not resourceful enough to manage a move to another place where better-paid employment may still be available.

Others are out of work because products such as textiles and shoes are now manufactured in other countries with far cheaper labor costs than in America. Until the economy shifts to absorb these people they are out of work. Many of these displaced workers are homeless and hungry.

There is another group among the homeless and the hungry, those with various kinds of mental problems. Public institutions have been releasing mental patients for outpatient care who may have a "home address" but really have no homes. They go to their families, but too often their families are not prepared to help. There is an awful syndrome of poverty, illness, illiteracy, and economic displacement that operates. One disadvantage feeds another and they all are synergistic. If you have one malady you are afflicted with them all!

These persons become no one's responsibility in particular and they are in the streets, easy victims of violent crimes, vulnerable to drug addiction and alcoholism and the concomitant criminal activity. One finds it hard to believe that such persons can exist in a society with a per capita yearly gross national product of over $13,000—compared to $120 for Bhutan!—and a military budget of $300 billion (Figures from John W. Sewell and Richard E. Feinberg, eds., *U.S. Foreign Policy and the Third World*; Transaction Books, 1985). It is incredible that the economy has no way of absorbing a half million mentally incompetent persons who cannot earn a livelihood and who do not qualify for other public support.

In the 1960s War on Poverty we discovered that 38

million Americans lived below the poverty line. When various programs were designed to meet their need, the general public was very begrudging. Somehow there was a feeling that everyone received what he or she deserved. All sorts of jokes and cynical public comments were made about the poverty program. It has become unpopular to be concerned about the poor.

Our culture has a Darwinian philosophy that promotes winners. The theory is that the reward is out there for the person who struggles for it. Of course, some are better able to win the reward than others, having inherited a strong, supportive family, good health, a sound mind, an adequate self-concept, and a happy childhood. So, whether rich or poor, they compete and succeed!

They become the winners. It appears that they did it all on their own until one looks at their advantages at the starting line. Others at the same line have poor health, a weak mind, or a disorganized and unloving family, a negative self-concept, a violent childhood. They have no idea of the reward promised them and even less idea of how to go and get it, if indeed the prize is there.

My childhood was spent in a small neighborhood in the Southeast where there was a constant influx of people from a nearby impoverished dirt farming area. Those who had some urban exposure were more street smart, more literate, and more aggressive. They had learned to imitate the mores and the life-style of their better-off urban counterparts and thereby gained an informal education in domestic service or working in commercial establishments. Those who worked around the better-off urbanites learned how to dress, to speak, to hustle, to save money, to drive an automobile, and other needed skills. They used these skills to make themselves marketable. The new arrivals, with mud on their heels, used poor grammar, spoke with an indistinct accent, wore farm clothing, looked lost, routinely accepted rejection, and stayed poor and marginal. One of my early recollections was the sympathy I had for the children of these immigrants and the way they were teased and called insulting names in school.

The preacher who is sensitive to community concerns will not wait for a crisis but will lift up the issue of the homeless and the hungry before the people as a matter that is illuminated and brought into focus by the good news of God. The gospel is primarily concerned with our care for those who are victims of illness and poverty. If Jesus returned tomorrow and picked up where he left off, he would pass by our Gothic, air-conditioned, cushioned sanctuaries and head for the public parks where the homeless find each other.

We are a free society, with a free economy and no coercion to compel anyone to surrender wealth to lift others out of need. This freedom permits us to be as callous, as begrudging, as stingy and hard-hearted as we wish. God forbid! But the same freedom allows us to become aware of where many began in life, and what their start was like. With our freedom we can canvass all of the options open to us to care for the homeless and the hungry, including the option to petition our government at whatever level, prepare a moral consensus, and seek a sane remedy.

The Priority of Education

Many of the crises that rise before us, that grab headlines and sound alarms throughout the community, are attributable to a growing uneducated underclass whose boundaries are hardening in America. Here is the source of much of the major drug distribution, teenage pregnancy, unemployment, and degeneration of scarce housing stock. One moves among the underclass, black, white, or Hispanic, and finds tenements are ill-kept, vandalized, and threatening. Persons with pride seek to live elsewhere. The stench of urine is sickening in every hallway and elevator, the police are making frequent drug busts, children are having children, and the schools are like jails. Good teachers flee these neighborhoods, reading scores are low, the dropout rate is high, graduation classes are small, and the crime rate is staggering.

Obviously, this situation is a source of bad news: babies falling out of windows, neighbors raping neighbors, car radios stolen for a fix, subway token booths robbed, policemen shot, teenagers stabbed, banks robbed, and old ladies killed for a welfare check. Politicians with no constructive answers point to these horror stories and campaign for the death penalty and bigger jails.

But when one visits neighborhoods that are clean, orderly, and prospering, the obvious difference is that people can read and write, and organize paragraphs, and reflect on ideas, and communicate, and criticize their environment, and examine options, and devise strategies for change.

We can either live with the crises—the sirens, the bells, the whistles—or we can focus on creating the kind of educational experience that is needed to breed a new generation. No magic wand can be waved over these conditions to make a change. We are dealing with persons with civil rights and with dynamic personalities. They will use their human potential for good or ill, for positive outcomes or negative ones.

Many churches in the toughest ghettos hold something similar to a baccalaureate service of worship, celebrating young people who finish high school, college, and graduate and professional schools. It is common to hear of ghetto children graduating from Yale, Columbia, Harvard, Penn, Rutgers, Smith, Wellesley, MIT, Dartmouth, and Brown. In the Abyssinian Baptist Church of Harlem are young alumni of all of these schools. The young people's choir director finished Brown, a soprano graduated from Mount Holyoke, and the minister of music has a Ph.D. from Rochester's Eastman School of Music, while across the street are a dozen apartment buildings, empty and gutted. One has to start somewhere. If the authorities are intransigent about renewing the environment, nothing prevents us from renewing the people within it! And everyone knows that enlightened people will not tolerate a decadent environment very long.

So if we make education a priority, soon the atmosphere will change and become inhospitable to the errant behavior, the violent tone, and the terrorized schools that create such bad news. It is better to spend money to reduce class sizes, hire tutors, and even provide residential institutions for those with no parenting, than it is to spend three times as much on a prisoner incarcerated in a brand-new jail.

No one knows this any better than a black adult who survived the segregated society of the deep South during the Depression. Poverty, ignorance, disease, and rejection pervaded the atmosphere. Self-hatred bred the worst forms of violence: ice-pick killings, hatchet slayings, and lye thrown into eyes. One felt sentenced to a short life in some of those dangerous, dusty Catfish Row hollows. But thank God for the schools, and for teachers who cared. A former teacher of mine still sends me a birthday card every year, even in my sixties! Such teachers were a part of our total existence, setting standards for human development and aspiration. In that environment my parents reared six of us. Among their children and grandchildren are nine who earned doctoral degrees, and several others are in process. Other families similarly situated, coming out of the same environment, have exceeded that record!

Education is self-renewing. Education breaks the cycle of generational ignorance and self-neglect. Education causes self-appraisal and self-improvement. Education enables one to participate in a social contract, to understand the limits of freedom, to appreciate a society of pluralism and openness. Education generates independence and self-reliance and is a contribution to society rather than a drain on it. We are not *giving* anyone anything when we induct her or him into the life of the mind. We are investing in the nation's future, enriching the culture, and eradicating a source of social failure. This is a second priority.

The Priority of Family Stability

The third priority is the nurture and strengthening of the family. In some quarters it is believed that the nuclear family is a relic of the past and that new sexual freedoms and new roles for women have made the family itself obsolete. But we are not dealing with something as negligible as the big fins on old Cadillacs, hand-cranked gramophones, castor oil, or paddle-wheel riverboats. The family cannot be made obsolete by common consent, because nature is the great given in this matter. Infants are born every day; they cannot be assigned to a committee.

Preserving the family is a high priority, and there is no concern more deserving of attention in our sermons. We are not speaking of pronouncing simple moralisms—*thou shalt* and *thou shalt not*—we are concerned about addressing this issue in the light of the good news of God. The good news is that God continued the marvelous act of creation, the making of a world, by instituting in it such wonderful processes as reproduction and genetics and cell development. As a part of this continuum God brought humankind all the way from a hairy, berry-eating, grunting nomad to *Homo sapiens,* with the big brain, the prehensile thumb, the computerized nervous system, and the capacity to create calculus, the subjunctive mood, and the great symphonies. God has given the human family the potential to produce a Gandhi, a Madame Curie, a Harriet Tubman, a Beethoven, an Edison, a Martin Luther King, Jr., for each generation.

So humankind does not take lightly this existence in families. One value that has evolved out of social experience, economics, psychology, and religious faith, learned from trial and error and commanded by God, is the importance of the family. The human infant, so richly endowed, requires a nest for development. The mother of humans does not swim or crawl or fly away and leave her infant as quickly as most other animals do because there is so much more that the human infant requires. The human father who wanders off to leave the mother in her crowded nest to defend and support herself alone, while he shrugs off the fact that he shared in the creation of these irreversible new lives and looks for other waiting females, to fill their nests also, is regarded as a failure and a disgrace, not the norm or the ideal.

Many of our community concerns can be traced to the erosion of the home and the fragmenting of the family. Those who visit prisons from time to time are struck by the fact that the vast majority of the inmates have never known a happy and loving home and the security and self-esteem that such a well-cared-for nest provides. Likewise, growing numbers of unwed mothers are themselves the children of unwed mothers.

The pressures on the family are formidable, but the most serious cause of its erosion is the popular notion that some alternatives are as good or better for raising children. This matter does not allow experimentation; if we guess wrong, the consequences are permanent, irreversible and cumulative. One generation of unparented, insecure, psychopathic children is all it takes to breed an unending procession of social mutants. This is exactly what has already taken place in some of our more desperate communities. A major, deliberate, and sustained effort will be needed to reclaim the family in many of these communities. This matter is a priority.

The women's movement has brought justice and recognition to half the population after shameless centuries of male arrogance and ignorance. The claims of women are overdue and justifiable. The challenge is to preserve the home, the family and the right of women to choose when, how, and for how long they prefer to maintain the nest for the young. So many have managed careers and also achieved high levels of success as mothers that it is useless to argue that careers and homemaking are mutually exclusive alternatives. There are all sorts of ways of keeping these options open. The sacrifice of the nest is not an option, however.

The demand of the gay population for recognition and acceptance is a matter of more serious moral ambiguity. On the one hand the good news assures us of God's love for all persons. But on the other, this love calls all to live in a disciplined relationship. Neither the homosexual nor the heterosexual has license to use another person purely as an object of physical gratification. Whatever it is that one person does with another sexually, the issue is the nature of the relationship. If two persons are taking the liberty to be sexual tools for each other, the relationship is sinful, destructive of personhood, and degrading, and no matter what we call it, it is sin. This has nothing to do with styles, tastes, trends, or preferences. The Christian view of persons precludes anyone's using another as an instrument, or agreeing *to be used* as an instrument, or entering a mutual relationship that accepts *only* the physical part of another person.

Indeed, many persons are not able to enter a full heterosexual relationship because of psychological, genetic, or social conditioning. They deserve unconditional friendship, compassion, support, and love. They are persons, children of God, and should not be patronized or indulged but accepted and appreciated without regard to sexual orientation. Beyond that, they are due every civil right that others enjoy and should not be deprived of such without due process of law. But when either homosexuals or heterosexuals want to advertise themselves on the basis of preferred types of sexual behavior, and want to be celebrated and recognized because of how or with whom they engage in sexual activity, we then encounter the dregs of human capacity and dignity.

It is a pity that movements that begin as a corrective, with the most salient purposes, become excessive and go beyond their intended objective. The labor movement began to save workers from the excesses of capitalists. Now workers have to be saved from the excesses of labor leaders who are abusing their offices for personal gain. The American black liberation movement that began in the thirties had by 1967 become perverted and embarrassed by young toughs burning black neighborhoods and looting liquor stores. The women's movement deserves our support and recognition, but we should be able to advocate women's rights without having to accept lesbianism as a necessary corollary.

The changing role of women, the acceptance of variant sexual preferences, along with high mobility, the rising costs of living, and the loss of religious authority in the area of sex and marriage have all contributed to the erosion of the family. The preacher must not allow these to become secondary issues; they must be addressed. The position of women and children in the light of the good news of God demands that we stay on the case of the preservation and nurture of the family. This remains a continuing priority.

We must make a choice: Are we going to preach *only* to crisis situations that are imposed on us by the media and the protagonists in the streets, or will we identify a few of the priority needs of the community and keep them before the people, to raise their consciousness, to provide support for agencies that deal with such priorities, and to give integrity to the work that we do for God as a herald of the good news?

Paul wrote to the Corinthians that his ministry was one crisis after another. The catalog of the events that threatened him included every conceivable obstacle, adversary, and danger to life and limb, and as he dealt with these threatening situations, one after another, he tells us he also had the care of the churches on his mind. Somehow we have to operate so that crises are met, but also in a way that sustains the nurture and guidance of the total spiritual lives of the people.

6

The Good News and the Quest for Community

Ye are the salt of the earth: but if the salt have lost his savor, wherewith shall it be salted? . . . Ye are the light of the world. A city that is set on a hill cannot be hid.
—Matthew 5:13–14

There are many kinds of community in which we participate and others that are known to us. And there are many degrees of community. Five large persons fitted into a taxi at an airport are in community—embracing a common goal or objective—but to a minimal degree. The objective of their togetherness is extremely limited, merely in the next hour or so to get from one point to another as rapidly and as safely as possible. Professional tennis players come from many countries, like Sweden, France, Germany, India, Czechoslovakia, South America, South Africa, the United States, and Australia. The president of their association was once a black player from Virginia, Arthur Ashe. Their bond is tennis, but beyond that they go their separate ways. That is a shallow though conspicuous form of community.

I recall visiting a small village in Assam, North India,

back in the early days following decolonization, 1953. I went to see a young missionary and his family from Altoona, Pennsylvania. He and his wife and children were happily settled among the people there, and the work was progressing beautifully. As we moved toward each other on the tiny airstrip, I raised my hand in a fist and shouted his name. We met with a hug and he said, "Man, it sure is good to see a white face again!" I am not white or near white! But I spoke "American" and I wore "American" clothes and I have an "American" greeting and it all came out of his mouth like a computer printout—White. The "American" community was one composite package. Moreover, that night, as we laughed about it, he could not remember that he had really said it.

We generally use the term "community" to refer to proximity, physical nearness, but persons often live and work near each other with very little else in common. There are *international* communities like the Warsaw Pact nations, the NATO alliance, and the United Nations with varying degrees of loyalty on the part of their members. There are *extranational* communities like the scientists and artists of the world, physicians and symphony conductors for whom national boundaries are negligible. There are some nations that are so culturally unique that they represent *national* communities, such as Japan, China, Burma, India, Nepal, Finland, or Liechtenstein with its 27,000 citizens.

In each instance there is a common bond: a shared ideology, a shared heritage or culture, or a shared set of values. In America we also have a national community, but it is more symbol than substance. We are a young nation, and some of our present national trauma may be the birth pangs of a genuine community coming into being.

We go to a baseball game as black, white, yellow, brown, rich, poor, Catholic, Jew, Protestant, Muslim, Buddhist, atheist, saint, drug pusher, gay or straight, educated or illiterate, and scream and shout together over something as inconsequential as a man with a stick hitting a ball wrapped in twine and covered tightly with leather. It looks like community, but the bond is entirely too thin and too brief. We share many values that are basic to our nation, such as one person, one vote; government by the consent of the governed; freedom of speech, press, worship, and assembly; and due process of law. We do not use armed force to bring about a change in government, and with a few notorious exceptions judges can decide a case and walk the streets unmolested. There are 250 million of us, and we trust our banks and our brokers, obey traffic signs, take our place in lines, pay our taxes on an honor system, and allow others to worship as they choose. These common aspects of our society indicate that we have the makings of a community and a residual set of common values even though we are a nation of great ethnic and cultural diversity.

The next step for us is to use what we have to cultivate a deeper, more genuine community, with the sharing of moral and spiritual values. Our Declaration of Independence and our Constitution rest upon acknowledged moral and spiritual values, and we are the envy of the world for having such lofty premises for our national life. Now we are challenged to transform a political state into a pluralistic, moral, and spiritual *community,* which can accommodate sectarianism.

Christian Practice in a Pluralistic Society

Of course, the Christian faith found itself doing much the same thing during the Roman empire, confronting a secular society with the good news of God in Christ. The faith became co-opted, however, and much of the good news was lost in the formation of a state religion. But in the United States, with our separation of church and state, the challenge is refreshing. Some would create again a church state, but another more viable alternative is before us. We can operate within our state, city, or town to influence this secular, pluralistic society toward becoming a genuine community. Those of us who believe the gospel and love our country need to find a way to share the good news on terms compatible with our pluralism and our separation of church and state.

This goal places a heavy burden on the churches, but it is worth bearing. Unfortunately, in the name of religion some of the most morally reprehensible acts against community have been committed, including soaking the earth with one another's blood by Christians and Muslims for three hundred years on a path from Gibraltar to the Syrian desert; John Calvin's consent to the burning of Servetus; the establishment and maintenance of racially exclusive "Christian" schools, religious hospitals, colleges, cemeteries, and prayer rails in America; and the carnage in Rev. Jim Jones's colony in Guyana.

Furthermore, Christianity has been diluted over and over, as a moral force, by those who were fervent in their profession but flaccid in their practice. John Newton, a slave trader who became widely known as the writer of the immortal hymn "Amazing Grace," before his dramatic conversion stood in a Liverpool church and thanked God for his recent success in trading trinkets and rum for kidnapped Africans and sought the congregation's prayers for future success. Likewise, William Wilberforce, who was vigorous in his abolitionist activities, nevertheless was adamant on the question of organized labor and allowed his faith in a blissful hereafter for the poor of England to blind him to their need for an improved standard of living in the here and now.

As we consider preaching and community concerns, one primary concern is to build on our marvelous political structure a community of shared values. Such a community will help us to overcome our ethnic xenophobia, our indifference to poverty, our idolatrous supernationalism, our destructive hedonism, our childish narcissism, and our competitive materialism. We are advancing technologically and scientifically, but much needs to be done to match that progress in our moral and social life. Many of the immediate concerns of our cities and towns are related to the need for a national awareness of the requirements of a genuine community. And without a conscious preference for a community of shared moral values we behave in the most tribal and instinctive ways, unworthy of our national charter and natural endowments.

Community and the Worth of Persons

What do we find in the good news that we can share with a pluralistic, secular society that may bring it closer to real community? Is the witness of Christ important? As we remain faithful to our own community in Christ, what do we have to share as citizens and participants in the larger secular society?

First, the good news stamps God's unique sign of worth and dignity upon each person in so indelible a way that no other person can claim the right to use anyone for his or her own purposes. This affirmation changed the direction of history. A lonely Simon, with sores covering his body, his toes and fingers eaten away by invading infections and his nerves numbed by leprosy, with no one allowed to be near him, nevertheless was good enough, clean enough, safe enough for Jesus to find room and board at his house in Bethany during Jesus' last week on earth. Jesus did not lodge with the high priest or the ruler of the Sanhedrin, not with any of the mighty or the powerful, but with Simon the Leper. There is our signal that every soul is precious in God's sight and that genuine community begins here.

I recall a hot day in Calcutta, India. It was harrowing enough to see the dead bodies hauled off every morning to be burned and to endure the stench from the pyre floating through the city. But beyond that were women and children, the crippled, the blind, the elderly, the hungry, with fingers as thin as pencils stretched out, begging all day long. And here were two of us, over two hundred pounds each, perched in a ricksha with an underweight boy about age eleven pulling us. It was too much. I had to stop him, climb down, and pay him the fare, double, to settle with my conscience. I know he needed customers and that if I did not ride someone else would have to. But I could not. The symbolism was too heavy for me. He was not in school; there was no other future for him. Presumably, he had accepted that he was permanently assigned to this status in life.

There are parts of New York City where young prostitutes beat on the car windows of male prospects, begging for a trick. They have settled for the notion that for money they will become mere meat, without soul, conscience, or mind. They will be only an instrument, like a guitar, a baseball bat, a pair of skis, or a ballpoint pen.

The good news is that Christ died for us all, the educated and the illiterate, the rich and the poor, the high and the low. We are all precious in God's sight.

This is a powerful message, because in a fascist state, or a materialist communist one, persons are the servants of the policies of the state. They have no recognized inherent rights. The basis of these rights in the United States is found in the Christian view of persons. The Declaration of Independence and the Constitution were written among people who honored Jesus Christ. Some leaders were deists, but the people were Christian. In the opening lines of the Declaration they acknowledged that the state did not confer human rights: these rights were endowed by one great Creator and could not be abridged or diluted by anyone.

Therefore, when we behave as Christians we demonstrate that all persons, including those with leprosy, muscular dystrophy, Alzheimer's, AIDS, cancer, dementia praecox, or any other disease, are fully endowed with their personhood. Whatever we do with them or for them must be done in the same way that we ourselves would want to be treated under similar conditions.

This principle lies at the center of our whole system of justice. At birth we are all at the same starting line, equal before God. But some immediately pick up better sponsorship than others—parents with higher income, neighborhoods with better schools, a life with infinitely better chances. Others, in their naked innocence, inherit a dirty, ill-kept home, unlettered parents, a slum neighborhood, and very pathetic life chances. How each one is served depends not upon differences in innate, intrinsic worth but upon obviously differing needs. This is the Christian contribution to the secular pluralistic culture, our estimation of the worth of persons. In our preaching we must advocate this basic approach to the building of community in a free, pluralistic nation. It is a prerequisite for a genuine community.

Community and the Losers Among Us

The second contribution that Christians can make toward community is to recognize the victims of social neglect and unfair treatment. The disciples of Jesus did not understand why he would want to stop on the Jericho road to listen to the plea of blind Bartimeus for help. His condition they took as given and final. But Christ would always move closer to the hurt persons of the world and show compassion. He did not believe that everyone had what she or he deserved in life. There were innocent victims all around him.

In our society we are surrounded by those who have not been able to benefit from this dynamic, creative, free enterprise system. The enormous opportunities in America require that one have ability, self-esteem, confidence, and persistence in order to take full advantage of them. And many do. Unfortunately, many of those who do cannot understand those who cannot—who do not have these characteristics. This is largely a question of inadequate information, on the one hand, and begrudging contempt on the other. One recalls the awful fight it took to get a minimum wage approved by Congress. We had grown accustomed to having a peon class of lawn boys, dishwashers, cleaning women, car washers, kitchen helpers, garbage handlers, chambermaids, errand boys, nannies, teenage car hops, soda jerks, stockroom porters, and launderers who had to take whatever we gave them, without regard to their needs or our ability to pay. With little education and no advocates, these persons remained at the survival level.

Christians are slow to see the Spirit of Christ in such

situations. In fact, today many Christians are altogether too closely identified with the political mentality that is most indifferent toward the poor. They offer
charity but fail to understand how inadequate it is to
pass out surplus cheese to the hungry and fail to create
jobs for them.

The good news is that God is in Christ, and this is
a liberating presence. It means release from psychological disorders, physical weaknesses, hunger and
thirst, and social ostracism, as well as release from sin
and guilt. It means the abundant life, life overflowing!
When a preacher presents Jesus as liberator, the need
for such liberation today becomes apparent everywhere. There can be no genuine community when
some of us are so healthy, well fed, comfortably
housed and dressed, well educated, and upwardly mo-
bile while others, created in God's image, live another
life entirely, barely able to survive.

We may not have the wherewithal to give everyone
what she or he may need, and it might not be best if
we were able to do so. But we need to be about the
business of finding practical and prudent ways of assuring that we do care for the needs of persons, that
we do try to make them independent and competent,
that we do try to get them on an escalator out of
poverty and open the door to the abundant life. One
cannot read the gospels and miss this point in Jesus'
teachings and examples.

We cannot guarantee equal achievement for all persons. We can only attempt to remove from their lives
the consequences of their disadvantaged birth, to get
them to the starting line without unearned weights
and impediments.

Most of us begin not at the starting line at all but
ahead of it, by virtue of having inherited enormous
advantages. These advantages may not be material. I

had a daddy who taught me to play the clarinet, who carried all six of us to Sunday school, who demanded homework every night, who required that we participate in housework and earn our pocket money at odd jobs. He taught us how to use planes, wrenches, and saws and how to care for paintbrushes and oil ball bearings. We left home well equipped for life, loving God, appreciating hard work, knowing Jesus, able to pray, saving money, pressing trousers, shining shoes, being neat and on time, reciting the psalms, understanding and using libraries, respecting authority, and with a healthy self-concept and compassion for the hurt and the hungry. What a package for children to receive!

Christians should know that no one can *earn* parents like that. Such an inheritance is the grace of God. With our knowledge that God loves us all equally, we begin to build community by recognizing the victims of neglect and trying to make the abundant life a possibility for them. This is our contribution to real community in a pluralistic society.

Commitment to Those Most Estranged

If this view and understanding of persons is the basis of community, we should be willing to assure that this attitude toward persons is not merely sentimental but that it is a commitment to action on our part.

Many years ago I learned something from foreign missions regarding the kind of action we can take. It is one thing to go among deprived people and preach Christ and baptize converts; it is quite another to equip them for changes that will bring about relief from their long-term suffering. Everywhere I went to visit missionaries I saw large crowds with no education, no medical care, no money, and no political leadership. These conditions meant interminable suffering and dependency. No community results from such an arrangement, only a continued master-servant relationship. But as a result of what the missionaries had been doing—building schools, infirmaries, and churches—one saw progress and human advancement. And later one saw agitation for independence and freedom.

A genuine community will not affirm full personhood and then fail to address the gross denials of personhood in the society. The preacher has a great opportunity to keep people abreast of these needs in an intelligent, resourceful way, keeping the light of the good news shining in all corners of our common life.

One of the awesome tasks before us is how to separate urban youth who are victims of a slum mentality, drug culture, and violent society from this motley legacy. Somehow this chain of cause and effect must be interrupted; an intervention of major proportions must take place. Otherwise we are engaged in a gross deception by making gestures of concern without getting at the gut issue. Jesus rejected such superficiality and dealt with persons where they were and how they were. He was "result" oriented. Because of his ministry a man could exclaim; "I *was* blind but *now* I see!" The moral earnestness that must accompany our tokens of love will bind us more closely into a meaningful community.

Such a commitment calls us to intervene effectively on behalf of young people who have no real parenting. They are many, with no real homes and no real adult guidance and care. We need to do something as dramatic as the Marshall Plan for Europe, the land-grant colleges for industry and agriculture, the G.I. Bill for World War II veterans, and the creation and defense of the state of Israel. We know how to intervene. We need to do so in a way that will break the chain of causation that has given us 500,000 young people with no parenting. The cost would be a fraction of the costs of new prisons, probation officers, and judges and the political fallout from the highly publicized street crime that now crowds the news. The price of neglect is already staggering, and the unit cost for such a program is feasible. It is also a chance to make citizens and taxpayers out of dependents, have fathers and husbands instead of addicts and recidivists, and restore personhood to those who behave like robots, at the mercy of their instincts and glands.

Compassion must become actualized. Genuine community calls us to go beyond sentiment and pity to intervene effectively. Community is not a frothy, pithy, perfumed gesture. It has grip, cleats, traction, results.

Preachers have to give support to ideas and plans that move us toward community in modern urban America. Our sermons must have muscle, intellectual and moral meat. If we are earnest about genuine community in America, after we blow bugles and shoot fireworks on the Fourth of July, and salute the flag and sing about bombs bursting in air, we must turn our minds to what America truly stands for. We must celebrate the idea of persons as ends, not means; we must redeem the victims of unfair treatment and create interventions to prevent further victimization. This is the basis for community.

Finally, what we contribute to a secular and pluralistic society is not a forced or an artificial unity, an assumed consanguinity, a coerced bond or affiliation. Neither are we into badges, special handshakes, passwords, or exclusions. We operate from the nexus of our togetherness in Jesus Christ and find our way into the world, bearing our witness and doing what Christ would have us do. But by the very nature of the voluntary consent that Christ invites we cannot compel conformity. Indeed, at best we are no more than the leavening in the loaf. There is in the community room for those at every level of success and attainment who share the values that bind the community together.

We bring to the larger society certain values that become a part of the culture, that affect our institutions, help to determine our social goals, influence political decisions, examine our national policy and posture, and set the direction for the unfolding future. Already in America we have seen Christians in the forefront of the antislavery movement, the women's suffrage movement, the civil rights movement, and the women's rights movement; in social service agencies, hospitals, and schools; and in the care of orphans and the aged. The laws of the land that have caused our society to be more humane and that have elevated our quality of life have had wide sponsorship, but in the forefront have been those whose values were shaped and formed by the good news of God in Christ.

The preacher is called to challenge the congregation to respond. He or she is called also to assume a continuous tacit, implicit, de facto guardianship of the abundant life, to possess the mind of Christ, and to reflect the good news of God in every aspect of our culture, through all its shifts and twists, contributing the good news to a community of moral and spiritual values.

Jesus said, "Ye are the light of the world." This means we should accept the role of moral and spiritual leadership and assume the initiative in providing the basis for a genuine community, in America and in the world.

7

Water for the Thirsty Soul

> As a hart longs
>   for flowing streams,
> so longs my soul
>   for thee, O God.
> My soul thirsts for God,
>   for the living God.
> —Psalm 42:1–2, RSV

Unless we are careful, we may find ourselves addressing community concerns on a wholesale institutional and political level, forgetting the individual whose life has been victimized and who needs personal attention. Do we have a message for victims of social failure? Our attention can become focused so completely on city hall, the police, hospitals, the penal system, schools, and gambling casinos that we may overlook the person who has borne the burden in a very private way.

The constant pressures of the society we have created are draining on the human spirit, and the demands of living a productive and resourceful life and avoiding economic dependency are not easy to han-

dle. The exhaustion that comes over us is undramatic
and hardly noticed by others, but a sensitive preacher
recognizes this thirst of the soul.

The Need for Living Water

Little wonder, then, that Jesus used the figure of
spiritual and even physical thirst to teach the most
important lessons we must learn. "Blessed are those
who hunger and thirst for righteousness, for they shall
be satisfied" (Matt. 5:6, RSV). "Whoever gives to one
of these little ones even a cup of cold water because
he is a disciple, truly, I say to you, he shall not lose his
reward" (Matt. 10:42, RSV).

In the Gospel of John, the fourth chapter, we find
Jesus responding to this very issue. He met a woman
at Jacob's well outside the Samaritan town of Sychar.
He was tired and thirsty at high noon and had no jar
or cup to let down into the well. So, in a neighborly
fashion, he asked the woman to allow him to drink
from her jar. And with that, the conversation went far
beyond a mere drink of water. The ensuing dialogue
revealed that she had a feeling of inferiority, a stigma
that she bore, a sense of diminished worth. She said
to Jesus, "How is it that you, a Jew, ask a drink of me,
a woman of Samaria?" Jews and Samaritans did not
mix. Suddenly, the gospel, the good news, was face-to-
face with the kind of tribalism, human alienation, estrangement, hostility, animosity that has been so
pervasive, so endemic, and so burdensome to the
human sojourn.

Before Jesus could even get to drink the water he
needed so badly he had to confront the issue of racism
and separation. Samaritans and Jews had lived in
neighboring areas since the days of Ezra and Nehe-

miah and the reconstruction of Jerusalem and the temple following the exile of the Jews into Babylon. Not all Jews were carried away by the exile. Some remained in the homeland. As is so often the case, the occupation army mingled with the local people and intermarried so that some of their culture and religion was mixed with that of the indigenous folk. In the eyes of pure Jews, this remnant left behind in Samaria became polluted. They were ostracized, denied communion, avoided, and for six hundred years left to worship at their own temple in Gerizim, not in Jerusalem.

Then, as the conversation proceeded, Jesus found that she not only bore the stigma of being a Samaritan but had been abused as a woman. She had been passed from one man to another, in a world that failed to regard women as having rights equal to men. She had had five husbands and was living with a sixth man. Those of us who counsel persons passing through the trauma of a broken romance or a failing marriage know how delicate this can be, and we try hard to lead them from this shaking, trembling ground to a safe place to stand. A woman invests much in childbirth and rearing infants, and becomes dependent on the support of a loyal mate. Imagine the trauma of five domestic hurricanes, the screaming and fighting, the name-calling, the lonely hours when life quiets down. She had been dragged through it time and time again.

She might have needed water for the thirst in her throat, but she needed much more than that. She needed the living water for her thirsty soul.

We are now looking at one of the most subtle community concerns that could go unattended as we pursue those that are more glaring and get more press.

And yet this concern, when overlooked, can be at the root of many others: alcoholism, drug abuse, battered spouses and children, divorce, suicide, and all of the accompanying pain. When there is a spiritual malaise and persons cannot command the resources for a remedy, life starts falling apart.

Among all the things we do as preachers, we had better be sure that week after week, whatever else may fail, we make available water for thirsty souls. This is a priority community concern.

One Sunday a well-dressed, energetic young woman came to greet me after the service. She said that she had sent a letter to me asking for an appointment. Her company was on strike, she had to cover the assignment of one of the striking workers, her son was goofing off in school, her car needed repairs, she could not get to her evening classes at night without her car, and all this was draining her. She was losing fast. She needed a resupply. But because I had preached on Paul's letter to his friends in Philippi about how he had found strength in Christ for anything, she had already been helped. So she asked to cancel the appointment.

Not all thirsting persons look to alcohol or cocaine as an exit. Even in urban settings where transportation is a problem, they have learned that it is worth getting up and getting ready on Sunday morning and making it to the place of prayer. Nothing else will do. They need to get a hold on the horns of the altar, to find asylum in the cleft of the great rock. What a blessing, then, to find the preacher ready with the living water. What is it about the living water that we need to emphasize to meet the needs of those who have come to us for refreshment and renewal? What can we expect to accomplish? How do we best state the case?

The Universal Nature of Spiritual Thirst

First, let us affirm that this thirst of the soul is indeed found among all people, as Jesus showed. Even Samaritans need a source of spiritual renewal! Life comes at all of us with the same trials, heartaches, dangers, toils, and snares. It matters not who you are; the givens of life—the basic ingredients of uncertainty, unfulfilled dreams, faded hopes, unscheduled tragedy—and its very brevity leave us with a thirst of the soul.

When the spaceship *Challenger* exploded in the skies over the unfathomable depths of the Atlantic, it was clear that the seven-member crew—two women, three white males, one Hawaiian, and one Black from rural South Carolina—was lost. They were all talented, scholarly, and skilled in their work. But in one split second, the color of their skin did not matter, the texture of their hair, their gender, their long experience in one social stratum or another, their economic status—none of this was significant before the awesome event of a giant spaceship hauling 500,000 pounds of liquid hydrogen that ignited and sent them to their abrupt and tragic deaths.

And the tears of sadness shed in Concord, New Hampshire, in Beaufort, North Carolina, in the state of Washington, and in Hawaii were all filled with pain, all just as briny, and flowing with the same throbs of grief in every living room, and with the same unashamed resignation. If you could have weighed, measured, or calculated the pain, the answers would all have been the same from each living room, black, white, or yellow.

Life does not discriminate; the thirst of the soul can be found among us all. In our mischief we have created and maintained all sorts of barriers and partitions, but beneath the veneer of culture and clan we are made of the same stuff of humanity. This one planet must accommodate us all with its limitations and opportunities, and the finite status assigned to us cannot be waived for anyone.

So at the core of life's concerns we are not that different, Samaritan or Jew, whether we worship at Gerizim or Jerusalem.

It was interesting how that woman reminded Jesus that the two of them had separate places of worship, her people at Gerizim and Jesus' people at Jerusalem. But he went further. He said that the hour was coming when it would not matter where one worshiped. What would matter was to worship in spirit and in truth. He never accepted the distinctions that had become important to her. He reached over and beyond them to talk about the living water that was available to everyone. Living water! What is it? A close communion with God through prayer and worship, a life of integrity with Christ and his leadership at the center, a satisfaction found in service to those most in need, a relationship with others marked by patience and understanding, a commitment to God that puts everything else in a subordinate position, an earnest search for community and reconciliation, for peace and goodwill among all people, an awareness of God's forgiveness and sustaining grace, a knowledge of God's presence and power, fulfilling all our needs and assuring us eternal life. All of these are included in the living water, available to everyone.

What Happens When Our Thirst Is Unquenched?

Not only do we all suffer from the same thirst of the soul, but if we don't find an answer for it the consequences can be disastrous. When our inner sources of renewal and hope have dried up, our defenses are weakened, our resilience is flimsy, our guard is down, and our coping capacity is limp. We need the living water.

There at the well with this Samaritan woman, Jesus found that her life was one big confusion. She had had five husbands and was living with a man unmarried to her. Most women will tell you that one husband is a gracious plenty; five must be a nightmare! We are not told of her other needs, but hardly can we believe that her life was complete otherwise. This string of husbands was probably the tip of the iceberg. We have heard nothing of her children, her illnesses, or her means of support and well-being.

Now we come to the crux of the matter. The gospel is vital to our response to community concerns. The victims of social failure are often those with the least capacity to rise above their circumstances. When poverty settles down on a family, the result can be defeat, resignation, adjustment to misery, and a slow accommodation to doing without. Or it can call up tough ways of coping, disciplined responses, canvassing of options, and eventual success.

I grew up in the Great Depression. Many were overcome by it. They had no living water within. But others looked poverty in the face and rose up against it. They had coping capacity. They had the living water. They found a second job, they made their own clothes, they stretched their food supplies, they planted small garden plots, they shared their homes with their kinfolk, they educated their children for a brighter day, they turned collars on worn-out shirts, put paper in shoes with thin soles, cut their own hair, made their own toys, hunted for used clothes, repaired their own cars, and survived with room to spare! Something within would not allow them to give up. They did not turn to alcohol or narcotics. These people I knew were church people, praying people, Bible-reading people, who knew all about the living water. They would tap their feet and clap their hands and sing!

> If the world from you withhold
> Of its silver and its gold,
> And you have to get along with meager fare,
> Just remember, in His word,
> How He feeds the little bird,
> Take your burden to the Lord
> And leave it there.

They would sing and pray as if everything depended on God, and then they hustled as if everything depended on themselves.

Redemption: Social and Personal

The underclass taking shape in our society is made up of persons who have been left behind on the ladder of success. Fragments of this underclass appear in every community. Their education is insufficient, their skills are out of date, their self-image is negative, their enthusiasm is low, their motivation is spotty and misdirected, their values are sketchy and in disorder, their money is short, their friends are few, their hope is dim. They live on public funds, are often in and out of jails and prisons, and have no strong family ties. Life for them is a drag. When we give them water for the thirst of the body, it is not enough; they will thirst again. They need to quench the deeper thirst of the soul. Because they are God's children, we must reach them and share with them the living water that we have found, that springs up within us, that gives us resiliency, drive, aspiration, and coping capacity. Their obvious and pressing physical thirst must be quenched. But unless we give them the living water, they will thirst again.

This underclass is growing, but it would be much larger and grow a lot faster if there were not some persons who are candidates for it who refuse to become a part of it. Some teenage mothers do go back to school. Some young drug addicts do kick the habit. Some dropouts do give school another try. Some street thieves do get jobs. Some semiliterate migrants from the worst pockets of poverty do take advantage of training programs and keep moving ahead. Where the public moral consensus fails them, and other initiatives do not reach them, they have to look within themselves for coping power. And many of them find the living water, springing up everlastingly.

In our large urban communities the difference is as plain as day and night: on a bright Sunday morning one sees the winners, the survivors hurrying into a big brick church to get started:

Praise God from whom all blessings flow

I've come this far by faith, leaning on the Lord.

And on every street corner are the victims of another kind of rearing, another kind of parenting, the losers. One of the most constructive approaches that the churches and their ministers can make in response to social concern is to begin at the beginning. Do not be ashamed of the gospel. When one has been victimized by social failure, the first need is for the living water.

Christ and Social Renewal

The answer for the thirsty soul is the living water, even Jesus Christ. And it is available to everybody.

The Samaritan woman went to Jacob's well to get some ordinary water to quench an ordinary thirst. But before she left she had found living water for the thirst of her soul. And it was not reserved for any special kind of people, but available to *any* thirsty soul.

In John 4:13–14, Jesus said to her, "Whosoever drinketh of this water shall thirst again: But whosoever drinketh of the water that I shall give him shall never thirst; but the water that I shall give him shall be in him a well of water springing up into everlasting life."

There are many needs in our society. We have done so poorly in equipping those who are marginal for survival and success. We have allowed our cities to decay where the teeming millions have fled, looking for a better chance. We have such disparity in incomes and opportunity; and sin being what it is, and greed being as chronic as it is, we can expect very little relief to be given on a volunteer basis. Our institutions of government will have to intervene with intelligent, constructive, prudent, and compassionate efforts.

But clearly, there are things that government cannot do. It cannot provide an inner source of spiritual renewal and resiliency. This is a spiritual issue that has all sorts of relevance for social concerns. The society that we want will require the best efforts, the best leadership, and the greatest compassion. But those who have catching up to do need to discover a source of renewal within—the living water of Jesus Christ.

This assertion may sound like a bromide until one finds a soul caught in the backwaters of failure, in the eddies of defeat, who cannot find the spiritual energy to survive. It may sound like a bromide until one realizes that there are millions of persons like that who know nothing of the living water. One could be tempted to call it empty pietism until one sees a struggling nation of people who are bogged down without a vital religion that has living water in it. With no ringing affirmation of human worth in it! With no knowledge of God's aggressive love in it! No cross, no Resurrection, and no living water. They are a people only partially what they could be. But find one who has the living water, and the difference is obvious.

Once during the time I directed the Peace Corps in Nigeria, a volunteer told me I had a friend near her school, deep in a rural area of western Nigeria. I visited that area with this volunteer and found a Yoruba chief who had graduated from Virginia Union University in 1911. He had gone back and settled down, and for fifty-one years he had taught and preached with no automobile, no running water, no electricity, no television, no library, no credit cards, no motels, no dentist nearby, and hundreds of people counting on him for legal advice, health counseling, farming suggestions, child rearing, and religious instruction and nurture.

There he stood, a very old man, with a broad and friendly smile and three deep Yoruba tribal marks on each cheek.

What on earth had enabled him to carry on? It was the living water within, springing up like a well of water into everlasting life. What it did for him in rural Nigeria it can do for us in the urban canyons of America.

8

Putting the Sermon Together

For we preach not ourselves, but Christ Jesus the Lord; and ourselves your servants for Jesus' sake.

For God, who commanded the light to shine out of darkness, hath shined in our hearts, to give the light of the knowledge of the glory of God in the face of Jesus Christ.

But we have this treasure in earthen vessels, that the excellency of the power may be of God, and not of us.
—2 Corinthians 4:5–7

When the preacher faces a congregation, every person out in front represents a unique set of problems, questions, needs, concerns, burdens, anxieties, successes, failures, and distractions. People do not wear signs. The preacher has to know them well enough to anticipate where they are. One may suppose that if they are like most congregations, many have come with an honest hunger and thirst for righteousness; others have come purely out of habit and tradition. Some have very special needs: a broken romance, an awful sin that needs to be forgiven, a big disappointment on the job, a child's report card that is an embarrassment, a death in the family, or simple spiritual exhaustion.

Before an audience like that one cannot go about raising a community concern without recognizing where the people are and, by the use of some well-thought-out method, preparing to lead them into a readiness to hear about such a community concern. Notice how Jesus always dealt with people in terms of their own experience as he led them into deep and profound truths: a certain man had two sons; a Pharisee and a publican went up to the temple to pray; a certain man was on the road to Jericho; a husbandman went on a journey to a far country; a man set out to build a tower. He took pains to enter their experience, their world. He taught, using ants, fishing nets, fig trees, snakes, rocks, seeds, weeds, birds, and lilies.

Likewise, if we are serious about preaching on community concerns, it is important how we begin. Let us assume we have a proposition or a theme in mind. We have arrived at this proposition by close observation and familiarity with a community concern, by an awareness of the moral consensus among the congregation, and by a commitment to the application of the good news of God to concrete situations. The sermon has an audience, and it is our task to communicate with that audience. So we must know not only the good news and the community concern but also what the disposition of the hearers may be.

We know already that there are deep religious doubts all through the place, some anger and alienation over a life that does not hold together, and all forms of idolatry: love that belongs to God given to cars, golf, food, travel, clothes, lawns, boats, degrees, money, and power. We cannot assume that everyone is eager and morally attuned to the will of God, waiting for our proclamation. We will be wise to assume that we must win their attention, create a level of interest, raise their consciousness on the matter, provide factual data, share our concern and commitment, and go for a verdict. That is some distance to cover, and it will require method as well as conviction.

Getting Started

A very helpful method comes to us from the German philosopher Georg Wilhelm Friedrich Hegel. He systematized a process of logical development that we use quite commonly. For example, let us assume I want to have a new car for my daughter Barbara's wedding. This wish is the *ideal,* my *thesis.* But here comes the *real,* or the *antithesis:* my present car is running well, I still owe money on it, a new car will carry higher insurance payments, and I still have to pay for Barbara's wedding. A new solution will not emerge unless the ideal and the real are identified and faced honestly. So I must ask the question: In light of these two truths, what solution will best take both into account? I decide to rent a shiny new car for the wedding day and continue to pay for the car I have and the wedding. That solution is the *synthesis,* which has come about from taking into account both the *thesis* and *antithesis.* Neither one alone would have led to this particular solution. This method, based upon Hegelian thought, is a good tool for preaching on community concerns.

In developing a sermon, we first settle on the thesis—the expanded statement of the main proposition to be set forth in the sermon. Next we identify the antithesis—the set of facts, the problem, the conditions that evoke the sermon in the first place. In the sermon outline, the thesis may be stated first as the *introduction.* It will set forth the good news of God as it relates to and illuminates the concern, in current and relevant language and thought. The antithesis, the statement of the reality confronted by the good news, then becomes the *transition* to the body of the sermon. Or for the sake of interest or clarity, the two can be reversed, with the antithesis presented first, in the introduction, and the thesis following in the transition.

For example, a sermon on the family could be developed either way.

> INTRODUCTION (ANTITHESIS, THE REAL): In America there are two divorces for every three marriages. Several social forces operating presently threaten the family as we have known it: mobility, new career opportunities for women, changing sexual mores, uncertainty about the role of the homemaker, an economy that compels both spouses to work, and the weakened influence of religious authority in the lives of people.

> TRANSITION (THESIS, THE IDEAL): But our understanding of the needs of men and women and of the importance of parents to child development calls for strengthening the family. The pressures that operate against the family can and must be dealt with, because the total needs of persons are best met in a stable, loving, and God-fearing family.

These could be placed easily in opposite positions and developed accordingly. The point to understand here is the function of the thesis: It responds to the antithesis and supports the positive claim that the sermon stakes out for itself in the proposition and the subject.

In other words, the antithesis states the real, the community concern, a set of facts that calls for action, a need that must be addressed, a fraud or a deceit that needs to be exposed, a trend that needs to be reversed. There is a reason, a motive, an interest, for preaching *this* sermon at *this* time. Whatever that reason, motive, or interest may be should be stated in the antithesis. The sermon is preached in response to it. The thesis, the ideal, is the meat of the response to the concern presented in the antithesis.

The thesis is a solid statement of the good news that draws upon 2,000 years of Christian witness and experience in the world and reflects the activity of God among persons as presented in the Bible (see chapter 3). It is informed by world history interacting with the history of Christianity; it appeals to evidence from the natural sciences that may bear on a given point; it canvasses the social sciences in the same way; and it leans most heavily on the knowledge and commitment of the preacher.

This presentation of the ideal in the thesis and the real in the antithesis leads us into the *relevant question*, a discrete, finite, candid question that limits and sets the parameters for the sermon. The illustration above regarding the sermon on the family could lead to any one of several relevant questions:

How did the family become so threatened?
What is the real case for holding on to the nuclear family?
If we lost the family, how serious would that be? What are the real consequences?

The more relevant the question, the better the body of the sermon. Any of these questions could lead to a fruitful discussion as a *synthesis*, the body of the sermon.

The skeleton of the whole sermon looks like this:

SUBJECT
PROPOSITION
TEXT
I. INTRODUCTION (antithesis), the real.
II. TRANSITION (thesis), the ideal.
III. RELEVANT QUESTION, to reconcile the real and the ideal.
IV. BODY (synthesis), the message, the resolution which answers the relevant question in two or three or four or perhaps as many as five or six points.

Many persons, knowingly or otherwise, not only follow this method in building sermons but also in ordinary conversation—in selling used cars, proposing for marriage, asking for a promotion, or planning a vacation. It is a way of thinking that facilitates reaching the truth. It pleads that nothing important should be overlooked or taken lightly. Many of today's most influential preachers use this method from time to time. There is nothing sacred about it, for it is only a tool, an instrument borrowed from the philosopher Hegel and put to the sacred use of the good news of God.

There are many other good methods, but because of the way in which the real and the ideal are presented for reconciliation, this method is especially useful when bringing before a congregation a community concern, an issue that may not be part of their daily routine or familiar in their social circle, and that may require them to act with confidence. The discipline in this method compels the preacher to deal with a community concern substantively.

Getting to the Body of the Message

When the preacher clears the desk and sits down to prepare a sermon, what, in order, are the steps to take in pursuit of this dialectical method? (Notice, this is *my* relevant question for this chapter!) I have already presented my subject (the construction of the sermon), my proposition (a well-thought-out method must be used), my antithesis (members of the congregation have many concerns, so the preacher must win their attention), and my thesis (the dialectical method is best for this purpose). Now follows the synthesis, the body of this chapter.

First, there must be a proposition stated in one sentence, one single driving message to be conveyed. It may arise out of Bible study that casts a ray of light on a community concern; it may be the outcome of an experience, a conversation, a television show, a book read recently, or a conference attended. Since the preacher strives to look at the totality of experience through the lenses of a Christian, and with the mind of Christ, there is no problem at all with where the inspiration for the message originates. However, it must be *one* message, finite and discrete, not a global topic or issue with ill-defined boundaries. There will be other Sundays!

This proposition, this message, should have a Christian thrust. Persons can get the day's current events from other sources, but they come to the preacher seeking the good news that comes from God. Therefore, *always* anchor the message in the witness of the Bible. This is the Christian's manual, and it should be given a central place. Hardly is there a brand-new situation that is not anticipated in the sixty-six books of the Bible. However, because the scriptures report on the long and varied relationship of the people with

God, there are parts that reflect very early stages of spiritual discernment and religious understanding. It is important to study such portions of the scriptures, but it is not necessary to preach on all of the murders, adultery, incest, and idolatry that may be found there. Neither can people benefit from the long genealogies and ancient religious taboos and sanctions, such as how to ostracize a leper, treat a woman in her menstrual cycle, brand a slave, or kill an Amalekite infant. There are parts of the Bible that show us clearly how far Jesus Christ departed from some of the tribalism and trivia of ancient Judaism. Much of it is hardly good news! And it is surely inept to drag unprepared people through scholarly debates on biblical criticism that leave them with more questions than answers. Whenever one ventures into such terrain the audience must be carefully equipped.

So the preacher is ready when a proposition, its biblical reference, and the subject are all in place. The proposition may or may not appear in the sermon, stated explicitly, but it should be written somewhere, near and visible for quick reference while developing the sermon. It is *the* message, aligned with the text.

Next, having settled on the proposition, a one-sentence "contract" for the sermon, and on the biblical reference from which it emerges or to which it is related, and having posted a subject to remind one of the "destination," it is time to go to work and develop the *thesis*, the ideal that reckons with the real. And it is time also to develop the *antithesis*, the real.

This part of the preparation will send the preacher to the library to refine the text, the biblical reference, as discussed in chapter 3, and to illuminate the Word. It is time also to become better rehearsed on the concern, the real, the issue that brings this sermon about, and to fortify the thesis, the ideal. Interestingly, however, this outline makes library work easy. (When the sermon is an oblong blur in the preacher's mind, it is hard to know where to start looking or for what.) Furthermore, there is something honest and creative about this method that discourages plagiarism or extensive borrowing. When one goes through this process, the sermon will bear the stamp of originality, whether it is good or bad.

When the thesis and the antithesis are all worked through, they will cover perhaps two fifths of the sermon. If the preacher is planning a twenty-five-minute sermon, not more than ten minutes should be consumed with the introduction (antithesis) and the transition (thesis)—or the reverse order, as one may prefer. There would then be fifteen minutes left for the body. Some may want to divide up the time differently or even lengthen or shorten the total time.

The sermon then moves from the transition, whether it contains the thesis or the antithesis, to the main body, the *synthesis,* by way of the *relevant question.* This question should be the most normal one that would naturally arise in the mind of the listeners when they have heard the real and the ideal set forth clearly. Generally, some *one* question that is more appropriate than any other should be raised to reconcile the thesis and the antithesis. If we don't raise it the people will do so after leaving church! It is *the* question that begs to be answered. The time spent agonizing over formulating the relevant question is worth it, because the body of the sermon will be the answer to the relevant question. For example:

SUBJECT: "Coping with Life's Ups and Downs"
PROPOSITION: Life is an uneven journey, and one must keep one's faith vibrant in order to cope with these unavoidable vicissitudes.

TEXT: "It is enough; now, O LORD, take away my life; for I am no better than my fathers" (1 Kings 19:4, RSV).

ANTITHESIS: God's prophet Elijah was not a weakling. He was a strong, rugged personality, who found himself experiencing the same ups and downs, successes and failures, low moments and highs that we all experience. And even Elijah, strong as he was, found himself overcome with these ups and downs from time to time.

Coping is not easy. It leaves many of us dependent on drugs and looking for other exits that create other problems [This is the real].

THESIS: What brings us through is the knowledge that God is aware of our situation. God was aware of Elijah's situation. And this faith will bring us through without falling apart [The ideal].

RELEVANT QUESTION: Is such faith available to everyone? Do you have to be someone special, with some special equipment or aptitude, to possess such faith? Does one have to be an Elijah?

Now, there may be a better way to go about that, but given that thesis and that antithesis the question raised is scorching with relevance! It will not be easily dealt with, but it is honest and poignant. Flowing from that question the following points may ensue:

1. Such a faith is first developed by being in fellowship with believing people. There is a contagious effect about a vital faith. Indeed, everyone can make this first step.
2. Next, faith is kept alive by your own walk through the Bible among faithful people. Meet Elijah and others over and over again.
3. By private personal communion with God, as revealed in Jesus Christ, and with the ever-present Holy Spirit, faith is made strong.
4. Finally, faith grows. It gets more and more mature as our spiritual experience ripens and mel-

lows. Coping capacity becomes more and more available to us.

Of course, having done all of this, one may still tear up the sermon and begin again. But often, halfway through, the Holy Spirit warms the heart and gives internal validation to the whole process. One often sees a tear of faith drop on the page without warning, along with perspiration.

The body of the sermon may follow many types of outlines: a logical progression, a historical development, or a theme expansion that reverberates like a symphony, amplifying the proposition in broader and broader relationships or deeper and deeper analysis. For example, a sermon on "Christ, the Firm Foundation" might reach the body, the synthesis, by answering the question, In what ways is Christ our foundation today? A *theme expansion* would be:

1. He is the foundation of our fellowship.
2. He is the foundation of our morality, our discipline, our way of life, our values.
3. He is the foundation of our hope.

A *logical progression* would go like this: How is Christ our foundation?

1. Because he was God's anointed Messiah.
2. Because he revealed God's truth in his ministry.
3. Because he revealed God's power in his death and resurrection.

A *historical outline* could go like this: How has Christ been regarded as the foundation of the church?

1. By training and empowering his disciples while in his earthly ministry.
2. By the guidance and direction of his Holy Spirit in the church through the ages.

3. By his presence in the lives of his servants.
4. By our hope of the consummation of history when he shall reign forever and ever.

All these outlines may flow from one proposition: The church in the world may be buffeted by modernity, materialism, nationalism, and hedonism, but it must rest on the sure foundation of Jesus Christ.

This method of sermon development holds all of the parts together. It saves the preacher from distracting the listeners with a miscellany of ideas and facts with no coherence, no real message, no theme. And no matter what the topic may be, this method is useful and sufficient because it approaches people where they *are* and delivers them to where they *ought to be.* There are no tricks here, no mirrors or magical blue smoke. It is the best way for one mind to communicate with another.

The antithesis is an honest, open, frank, concerned presentation of the *is-ness* of things. Therefore it is especially appropriate as a preparation for the statement of the *ought-ness* of things. In dealing with the question of the good news and community concerns, this method compels one to spell out the concern in a strong antithesis and then reply to it with the good news, the thesis. And in order to get at the details of the application of the good news, the relevant question compels the sermon to respond with a coherent outline in the body, or synthesis. Here is a sample outline on the text and proposition used above directed toward community concerns.

Christ the Firm Foundation

TEXT: 1 Corinthians 3:11 "For other foundation can no man lay than that is laid, which is Jesus Christ."

INTRODUCTION (ANTITHESIS): The church seems to be impotent in effecting results in dealing with many of the most critical community concerns. Our commitment is weak, our resources limited, our influence eroded, our voices are muted.

TRANSITION (THESIS): But the power of the church lies in its foundation, Jesus Christ, and the power of God that is available to us in Christ. Paul had to remind the church at Corinth that its problem was in rejecting its firm foundation in Jesus Christ.

RELEVANT QUESTION: What can we expect of the church when it stands firmly on the foundation of Jesus Christ?

1. We can expect a higher standard in the treatment of the weak and the powerless. Jesus was always elevating the condition of the losers of the world.

2. We can expect Christ to change our attitude toward others who are different. He reached out to persons beyond his own race and religion.

3. Finally, Christ challenges us all, whatever our position or responsibility may be, to follow him in reflecting the love and the peace of God in every situation: in the home, where we work, among our neighbors, in our unions, in our politics, and in our use of our time, our means, and our energy. Redeemed, enlightened, disciplined, believing Christians, possessed with the love of God, are a blessing to any community in whatever capacity they serve—as teachers, social workers, merchants, politicians, mothers, fathers, artists, physicians. There is no greater resource for any community than persons standing on the firm foundation of Jesus Christ.

The body may contain two, three, four, five, or six points. Too many points leave people confused; too few may deal with the question inadequately. Three or four seem best. The more serious question is how to develop them. I believe that these points, just like the introduction and transition, deserve full treatment. If each point takes approximately five minutes, there is time enough to support the point first from a purely logical or rational point of view and then from human experience, from the biblical record, from the history of the faith, or from the life of a person, first-hand or in literature. But by all means, the point is not finally developed until the testimony of the good news, as known and believed by the preacher, has crowned it. However they are organized, each point should be supported from several sources.

Notice, I have not mentioned a conclusion. When one has pursued an outline in any sequential fashion, the last point is *conclusive*. There is no need to take off into superficial flights of oratory and spoil a good sermon. It needs no further ornamentation. When the sermon is completed it is automatically concluded.

How all of the parts of the outline are put together in the final form is largely a matter of taste and temperament, letting God use you as seems best. The reality is that there are real people out there, and there is no reason for preaching at all if they are not to be reached. The method of sermon construction presented here invites the preacher to deal with the minds and hearts of the people forthrightly and honestly.

Suggested Reading

Boesak, Allan A. *Comfort and Protest: Reflections on the Apocalypse of John of Patmos.* Philadelphia: Westminster Press, 1987.

Coles, Robert. *The Moral Life of Children.* Boston: Atlantic Monthly Press, 1986.

Cone, James H. *For My People: Black Theology and the Black Church.* Maryknoll, N.Y.: Orbis Books, 1984.

Fuchs, Victor R. *How We Live: An Economic Perspective on Americans from Birth to Death.* Cambridge, Mass.: Harvard University Press, 1983.

Hebblethwaite, Brian. *Christian Ethics in the Modern Age.* Philadelphia: Westminster Press, 1982.

Kelly, George A. *Politics and Religious Consciousness in America.* New Brunswick, N.J.: Transaction Books, 1984.

Macquarrie, John. *Three Issues in Ethics.* New York: Harper & Row, 1970.

Mitchell, Ella Pearson, ed. *Those Preachin' Women.* Valley Forge, Pa.: Judson Press, 1985.

Outka, Gene. *Agape: An Ethical Analysis.* New Haven: Yale University Press, 1976.

Pifer, Alan, and Lydia Bronte, eds. *Our Aging Society: Paradox and Promise.* New York: W. W. Norton & Co., 1986.

Shinn, Roger L. *The Sermon on the Mount.* Philadelphia: United Church Press, 1962.

Shriver, Donald W., Jr. *The Lord's Prayer: A Way of Life.* Atlanta: John Knox Press, 1983.

Smith, Kelly Miller. *Social Crisis Preaching.* Macon, Ga.: Mercer University Press, 1984.

Thurman, Howard. *For the Inward Journey.* New York: Harcourt Brace Jovanovich, 1984.

Watley, William D. *Roots of Resistance: The Nonviolent Ethic of Martin Luther King, Jr.* Valley Forge, Pa.: Judson Press, 1985.